Expecto

An Essay towards

A Biology of the World to Come.

F. S. M. BENNETT,

Dean of Chester.

With a Foreword by Professor J. Y. Simpson,
of New College, Edinburgh.

CHESTER ;
Phillipson and Golder Ltd.
LONDON :
Simpkin, Marshall & Co., Ltd.
1926.

In token of gratitude for long friendship and of admiration for his work for the Church in the Principality I dedicate this book to the Most Reverend the Lord Archbishop of Wales.

Foreword by the Professor of Natural Science, New College, Edinburgh.

———

The Dean of Chester has asked me to write some words of preface to this book. His generous appreciation of the work of other men would make it ungracious to decline his request in any case. But to comply is indeed a pleasure, even if one feels that nothing can be added thereby to the value of the book. For the Dean makes it manifest that he is dealing with a question that is of urgent reality to him, and his earnest desire is to bring his readers into a state of mind in which they shall feel that its consideration is not merely the most natural of interests for them, but one with regard to which their decision must have a determining effect upon their every-day life, even as that life in turn influences their eternal destiny. His argument is broadly based, and there is a wholeness and continuity in the presentation of his thought that leads him to include something of the best of the thought of the past on the great topics of God and the world, of Man and immortality, in his modern and appealing presentation. At many points, as in the treatment of prayer, our Lord's attitude to His own works, error in evolution and so forth, the reader will be quickened by fresh and suggestive contributions. In a double aspect the book is concerned with Restoration—the restoration of the spirit of man, and the restoration of a noble edifice, within whose walls human lives have come into contact with the spirit of the living God. I would dare to express the hope that this twin endeavour, so full of vision and of heart, may have an abundant issue.

J. Y. SIMPSON.

New College,
Edinburgh.

PREFACE.

My book is greatly honoured by a foreword from Professor J. Y. Simpson, who most kindly read through its proof sheets and pointed out one or two inaccuracies which I have hastened to correct. He wisely refrained from comment on my speculations and I should be surprised if he agreed with them all. Indeed I shall be surprised if any of my readers agree with all that I have written. If some of it interests some of them, I shall be very glad, and if some in consequence buy and read some of the books to which I make frequent reference, I shall have done them a very good turn. If it adds to my correspondence I have an indefatigable secretary, who kindly put together the index for me

It was once wittily said of a sermon, which took a very long time to get to a very small point, that the portico was too large for the building. Perhaps a book, of which the four main chapters are the portico and only part of a single chapter, the building, merits the same criticism. But in this case it is only the portico that we can actually traverse and my chief object is to bring my readers through it to the door which admits to the building beyond and to persuade them to look through that door for themselves. On themselves must depend most of what they see.

I look myself into an immense building, of which through the door only a small part can be seen; but that part—like almost any part of a Gothic Cathedral—reveals enticing vistas of further wonders and beauties without end; while just inside the door are many friends.

It comes natural to me, as a Dean, to think in terms of a Cathedral, but thoughts will probably shape themselves differently for many of my readers. If so, so much the better perhaps; the great thing is for each to see as much as he can and in his own way. Those, however, who buy a copy of this book, will not be able to disassociate themselves altogether from our Cathedral of Chester, since all profits from any sale of this book will go towards the £1,250 still needed to complete a great work of restoration, which has made a large hole in twenty-five thousand pounds.

Where italics occur in quotations the italics are mine and where occasionally short sentences are placed in inverted commas without a page reference, they are nearly all taken from Professor J. Y. Simpson's *The Spiritual Interpretation of Nature* and *Man and the Attainment of Immortality*, which suggested a great many of the ideas elaborated in this book.

Chester Cathedral Parlour,
The Ascension, 1926.

CONTENTS.

	Page
Introduction	1
The World we live in	29
Organic Evolution's Mental Concomitant ...	59
Through Christian Telescopes	85
Along the Curve	119
Expecto	151
Index	171

of the great World Factory—Self Conscious Persons —was in the end going to be scrapped, there would be neither sense or meaning in the whole thing." That the universe is reasonable is a necessary and fundamental assumption of science. Certainly some sort of personal permanence is requisite, somehow, somewhen, and somewhere, if that part of the Universe which we know best, is to share in the rationality of the whole. I say "some sort of personal permanence." This is not, of course, the same as saying that human souls are inherently immortal. Nor does the rationality of the Universe depend on you or me surviving the grave. But we are, I think, bound to believe that some persons, as the final outcome of our World Factory, must be going to be permanent, on the same sort of ground as that on which some physicists believe that there is an ether of space. The Universe cannot be explained rationally otherwise.

I was thinking of taking for the title of my next book, if it ever got written, the phrase *An Immortable Individual*, coined by Professor J. Y. Simpson in his *Man and the Attainment of Immortality*. It exactly describes what I believe my readers and myself to be. Had I chosen it for my title, it would have signalised my indebtedness to the Professor of Natural Science at New College, Edinburgh, whose books, with those of his brother Professor, J. Arthur Thomson, of the University of Aberdeen, have helped me more, I think, than any other modern books to reach what is for myself at any rate, a more or less consistent and satisfying life-outlook. If, indeed, I had called my book "Professors Simpson and Thomson through a Parson's Spectacles," it would have been an accurate title. I hope that they won't think that my parsonic spectacles have altogether distorted them. It would have been an accurate title. But, alas, accuracy is seldom popular, and actual experience has taught me that on the popularity of their titles more than upon anything else, depends the sale of little books. Hence to *Expecto* I have audaciously added *A Biology of the World to Come*. I have often been guilty myself of buying a half crown or even a three and sixpenny book because its title caught my fancy, to find afterwards that the contents had as little to do with the title as many an indifferent sermon has to do with an admirable text.

So *Expecto* let it be—the first word of the Latin version of the last and most majestic sentence of the Nicene Creed—"*I look for* the resurrection of the dead and the life of the world to come."

II.

With *Expecto* for my title, instead of Professor Simpson's suggestive phrase *An Immortable Individual*, I proceed to borrow a sentence from him to describe the gist of my book. Thinking of the far distant past, with which such sciences as geology, palaeontology, and biology deal, he writes:—"It is not that we know exactly how things did actually occur; but by extrapolation of the curve of our knowledge we can reconstruct within the range of conceivability, if not of probability, the course of events." Once get a bit of a curve, and you can follow along the direction of its circle and see where it gets to. Geology extrapolates or extends *backwards* the curve of our actual knowledge regarding various forces playing upon the surface of our earth to-day; biology does the same thing with its knowledge of present-day conditions and characteristics of life; both are doubly rewarded. All sorts of items of evidence crop up to corroborate resulting theories and explanatory light is thrown, for instance, on sundry and manifold fossil remains in the strata of the earth and upon otherwise inexplicable survivals in the "stuccoed-all-over-with-quadrupeds" body of a man. May we not reasonably hope that if we extrapolate *forwards* this same curve of scientific knowledge (by which I mean, with Professor Simpson, "systematised knowledge in which the personal equation has been eliminated") we may be doubly rewarded in this direction also? If, through Christian telescopes, we follow along our curve aright, we ought to come across items of evidence in the deposits of our Scriptures corroborative of any resulting theory and to find fresh light in explanation of some of those incidents recorded in connection with the life of Our Lord on earth, which puzzle many minds and which some modernists seem anxious to explain away.

This is exactly what has happened as far as Professor Simpson has himself ventured to extrapolate the curve of his scientific knowledge forward, just as it happened thirty years ago when, under the title "*Natural Law in the Spiritual World,*" Professor Drummond wrote a book to answer the question:—"Is there not reason to believe that many of the Laws of the Spiritual World, hitherto regarded as occupying an entirely separate province, are simply the Laws of the Natural World?". It was indeed Professor Drummond who first set me thinking along the lines which have led to the following similar but in some particulars more adventurous and perhaps less acceptable speculations.

The Liverpool Diocesan Board of Divinity did good service recently when it published the Archbishop of Armagh's *Science and Creation*. On the second page the Archbishop writes:—"It is important to note that this scientific restatement of universal history is now passing beyond the lecture room and the learned journal, and becoming the possession of the multitude. This being so, it is a very serious matter that, to the average mind, Christianity in all its varieties seems to cling to an outworn view of the origins of things. It is true that among the educated the Christian creed is no longer thought to require the old interpretation of the Book of Genesis. But this is not enough. The situation demands something more than an apologetic. *If the scientific view of the history of the world be even approximately true, it should be, not a difficulty to be explained away in the terms of an ancient theology, but a source of light giving a new illumination and a fresh meaning to our faith.*" (The italics are mine).

I can see no reason why such "new illumination and fresh meaning" should not be forwards as well as backwards, and I think that every word that the Archbishop writes is true. It is incredible that our amazingly increased knowledge about what has been and about what is, should have no light to throw on what is yet to come. My own conviction is that when Science takes as much pains to forecast the future, by extrapolating the curve of her knowledge forwards, as she has taken pains to recast the past, she will find the prospect as attractive as the retrospect has been interesting. Already among her leaders of to-day she has pioneers in this direction. "I believe," wrote one of them quite recently, "that our present physical knowledge, when properly grasped and accepted, constitutes a beneficent source of power, of fertilising influence, a body of illustration and parable, which can be drawn upon and used by those whose business it is to deal with still higher things. Their congregations may not know enough, they themselves may not know enough, to utilise ascertained facts to the full. If they did—if only they could apprehend a tithe of what is now known by specialists—their teaching would be suffused with a dominating sense of Reality, in the strength of which they would press forward with an energy and enthusiasm such as were aforetime evoked in one to whom a great experience had been vouchsafed, and who continued not unmindful of the heavenly vision."*

It is perhaps in the field of Physics—a field in which Sir Oliver Lodge speaks as a master—that recent discoveries have been made which must cause us ultimately, and ought to cause us soon, to revise all our traditional views of the relation of spirit to body and of mind to matter.

Some there are, I know, who will be inclined to say, with no less a prophet than Bishop Westcott, that "We know too little to be able to form theories as to the world to come." "Scripture," he adds, "does not encourage us to enter on such an effort. The reserve of the prophetic and apostolic writings as to the unseen world is as remarkable as the boldness with which uninspired teachers have presumed to deal with it." The words occur in his "Historic Faith," a book which has been my *vade mecum* for years. The view he there expresses, and the views of those who think with him, are worthy of all respect. Yet it seems to me that, holding in mind together both retrospect and prospect, we do well to think once again. I have heard many a sermon and have preached some too, on or near Septuagesima

* Sir Oliver Lodge. "Ether and Reality," page 21.

Sunday, in which it has been pointed out, in connection with the reading of the first chapters of Genesis, that the Bible was written "that we might have hope" and not to teach us science or to save us the trouble of finding out anything that we are competent to find out for ourselves. Manifestly this is true of all that has to do with the world that lies behind. May it not, indeed must it not be true also of the world that lies beyond? Is there no ground for some legitimate disappointment that during the course of all these centuries we have made so little progress in knowledge of any future life and that in it to-day so few people seem to take much interest? May there not be in this direction, too, much that has not been revealed because we are competent to find it out for ourselves?

III.

Dr. Fosdick begins the stimulating and suggestive little book he has written for the Student Christian Movement, under the title *"The Assurance of Immortality,"* with the following paragraph:—"One of the most noticeable contrasts between this generation and those immediately preceding it, is the relative unimportance of the future life in the thought of the present age. When our forefathers were at all religious, and often when they were not, they not only took for granted the fact of continued existence beyond the grave, but they regarded it as a matter of supreme concern. . . . . Our fathers, therefore, hardly could have understood the present generation's scepticism about the truth of immortality; much less could they have comprehended that modern nonchalence which speaks and acts as though it made but little difference whether or not men live beyond the grave."

He goes on to give some reasons in explanation, some scientific, some social, and some illustrated long ago by Our Lord's parable of the seed sown among the thorns. The reasons he names are all contributory. The principal reason, however, is I believe to be found in another part of the same book, where a view of things is expounded which seems to be Dr. Fosdick's own. If I held such a view, I should find it very difficult to take any sort of rational interest in the life of the world to come. Dr. Fosdick himself has managed to survive his own view, or he would never have written his book. "When one considers," he says, "the utter inconceivability of a world in which we have never been, whose circumstances by the necessity of the case are alien from anything that we can dream, it is not simply probable, it is inevitable, that all our thoughts of the future are more unlike the facts than a child's house of blocks is unlike the Taj Mahal. Wooden blocks and marble minarets are at least in the same plane of existence, but this world and the next are unimaginably different."

If the next world is so altogether inconceivably different from this, I do not see how you can even begin to think about it at all, and, if you cannot even begin to think about it at all, I do not see how you can be much interested in it. It is, I believe, just because they do not know how or what to think about it, that so many of our generation have lost their interest. Our fathers thought that they did know what to think about it, and that was why they were really interested.

Dr. Fosdick discharges this monster gun—the recoil of which seems to me more dangerous than the projectile—at a position which calls for judicious survey and strategic capture rather than for bombardment. "In how many minds," he asks, "is life beyond the grave so intimately associated with special ideas as to the nature of the future world that, by a lamentable *non sequitur,* men deny immortality because they can no longer hold their old ways of conceiving it. The setting is rejected and with it the diamond is thrown away."

The question is very much to the point and the answer is that a great many people are acting in this very foolish way. But it would be an equally obvious *non sequitur* to suppose that because our forefathers formed impossible conceptions about the world to come, therefore the world to come is inconceivable. Our forefathers conceived that the earth was flat and stationary. We have learnt that it is round and in motion. We have replaced wrong conception by right conception, and, *mutatis mutandis*, this is just what we need to do with regard to the world to come.

Until we do form some conception of it which is compatible with the world, about whose past and present we do know a good deal, masses of people will continue to concern themselves not at all about that which they cannot at all imagine.

The obsolete conceptions about the world to come, which satisfied our mediæval forefathers and which do not satisfy us, are not more obsolete than conceptions that they formed about the world that is, and about God the Author of it. In forming, however, their conceptions of the world that is, of the world that is to be, and of God Himself, they did occupy a position which we very much need to recover. They thought about all three *in the same sort of way*. We do not think about all three in the same sort of way, and that is why we get into such puzzles and confusions.

To the men of the Middle Ages the world, in which they lived, was much more inconsequent and in some ways much more exciting than it is to us. All sorts of odd and unexpected things might happen. You could never be sure, for instance, what a pollarded willow or elm tree might grow into. They were, of course, as aware as we are of certain great regularities; but they expected strange and unaccountable things to happen and they happened with delightful frequency. When they thought about God, they thought about Him in the same sort of way; or perhaps it would be truer to say that they formed their conception of the world directly from their conception of God. The Majesty of God seemed to them to require that He should exercise the powers of an autocratic and unaccountable sovereign. A statement like "Just as a varying multiplication table would be the destruction of mathematics, so would a varying law of Nature be the destruction of the universe," would have seemed to them almost blasphemous. They did not try to think about the world, in which they lived, in one sort of way and about God, Who made it and rules it, in another sort of way. We do, and get ourselves into no end of perplexities in consequence.

Our mediæval forefathers, likewise, thought in the same sort of way about this world and about the world to come. In his *Ingersoll Lecture* on *Human Immortality*, William James writes:—"For our ancestors the world was a small, and—compared with our sense of it—a comparatively snug affair. Six thousand years at most it had lasted. In its history a few particular human heroes—kings, ecclesiarchs, and saints—stood forth very prominent, overshadowing the imagination with their claims and merits, so that not only they, but all who were associated familiarly with them, shone with a glamour which even the Almighty, it was supposed, must recognise and respect. . . . . . The whole scene of eternity never struck the believer's fancy as an overwhelmingly large or inconveniently crowded stage." Always picturesque thinkers, they pictured the world to come with amazing realism and congregations could see in colours above the chancel arch of their parish churches or in the windows behind and around them, what lay in store for the evil and the good.

The point I want to make is that, while many of their conceptions of this world and of the world to come and of God Himself were exceedingly crude, they were the same sort of conceptions, congruous conceptions. For them in consequence there was little or no cleavage between the sacred and the secular. Humour did not seem to them improper even in Church. They expected to find and they found God everywhere. Their religious thinkings and their scientific thinkings (as far as they had any) were expressed in the same sort of language and were conceived under the same sort of categories. What ever we may think of its particulars, their general position was as sound as it was sensible. I doubt if we need anything more urgently or more obviously than to recover it for ourselves.

IV.

Nor is it difficult to state in outline how it is that we have vacated this really sensible position and have come to think in one sort of way about the world that is, in quite another sort of way about God, and in no sort of way at all about any world to come.

As far as this world is concerned our knowledge has during recent years grown by leaps and bounds. Alike its immensities and minutenesses stagger us. We cannot help perceiving that it is a world of law and order. The uniformity of Nature is the basal assumption of all Science. It is Science's great and necessary initial act of faith. To express what we have discovered about the world, we have had to make what is practically a new language. It is, of course, perfectly true that a law of Nature is simply "a generalised statement, a conceptual shorthand report of Nature's observed uniformities of action," but the cumulative effect of such laws has been to change our whole outlook upon the world. Professor Simpson puts what has happened into a crisp sentence:—"The Universe on which we look out to-day is a dynamic Universe, in contrast with the static Multiverse that occupied the attention of previous generations."

It is the business of Science to discover and to formulate: it is the business of Religion to conserve and transmit. Science is radical and ought to be so: Religion is and ought to be conservative. The "static multiverse" idea left any amount of room for particular evidences of God in the world: but the idea of a dynamic universe, evidencing a reign of law, seemed at first to leave no room for Him at all, except here and there in such gaps as human knowledge had failed to occupy. Most of us, happily, have long since given up putting our trust in gaps and recognise that a perfectly orderly Universe, compelling us to see in it development and purpose, is more cogent and impressive as evidence than any number of particular happenings. But there is still at least an element of truth in Mr. E. T. Brewster's statement in his "*The*

Understanding of Religion" that "our traditional theology rests on an astronomy, which we have not believed for two hundred years and shall never believe again. Therefore our religion hangs in the air. That is in no small part what is the matter with us." To-day Science and Religion talk an altogether different language, and often mean the same thing without knowing it.

Even when we do attempt to follow out, in consonance with what we know about the world, the main thoughts suggested by our Creed, as to our belief "in God, the Father, the All Sovereign, Creator of heaven and earth," it cannot but be, as Bishop Westcott says, "that we find ourselves lost in unsearchable mysteries. The action of providence is so complicated and on so vast a scale that in our endeavours to follow it, we commonly do no more than isolate a few events from the broad stream of which they are a part . . . . As we learn more of the weakness of our own powers, more of the vastness of history, more of the unvarying forces of nature, God the All Sovereign the Creator, seems to be withdrawn further and further from us."

Much the easiest plan is to keep our scientific thinkings about the world in one compartment of our mind and life, and to keep our religious thinkings about God in another. Much the easiest plan, and a very common plan; but a bad one. In consequence and to our great loss, we draw a line between what we call sacred and what we call secular, which certainly our mediæval forefathers never felt themselves obliged to draw at all: our ordinary life is secularised and much of our religion loses reality. Someone has said (Principal Forsyth, I think) with terse truth, that the cure for pulpit dulness is reality. It is the cure for every sort of religious dulness, and much of our religion is dreadfully dull. It fails to grip because it has lost reality.

In a recent and most admirable call to prayer, signed by a number of thoughtful men, who had themselves prayed much and thought much before they wrote, occurs this passage:—"We who write this letter feel constrained to admit—and we take on ourselves our full share of the shame of such an admission—that at bottom what is wrong is, throughout the Church, our weak sense of God, our weak hold on Him, our weak faith in Him. Weakness *here*, at the very springs of life, is bound to spell weakness throughout the whole range of the Church's work and witness."

A weak sense of God is inevitable as long as we think of God in one sort of way and of the world in another. Our forefathers saw the hand of God everywhere in special happenings of all kinds; we too sometimes see His hand in special providences. Fortunate escape from imminent accident in a train would seem to bring Him very near to some of us. But the sort of thing that we need, in order to make God as real to us as He was to those who lived a few hundred years ago, is the recognition that every stroke of the engine's piston is evidencing the orderly wisdom of God: His is the energy of the steam, and His the wisdom that determines that all the world over, water at such and such a temperature in such and such a space shall always and every where exert with utter exactness so many pounds of pressure on so many inches of surface.

Thus to readjust our ordinary ways of thinking is doubly difficult. It is difficult with the difficulty which any change of any sort of habit involves, and it is difficult because it means finding the world's witness to the God Who made it, in just those very aspects of it which seemed at first sight to push Him further and further away. Orderly uniformity—a reign of law—what room is there here for the freedom of God the All Sovereign?—The answer of course is "all the room in the world." It is because God is perfectly free—using that great epithet in its only true sense—that the physical world (presumably the only sort of world in which free personalities can be developed) is rigidly determined from end to end. "Perfect freedom is perfect self-determination from within as opposed to rigid compulsion from without." If God was thought of as having made the best world He could out of refractory material, material which limited Him from without, just so far there would be signs of disorderliness and just so far the Maker of the world would not be perfectly free. The uniformity of nature is the only possible counterpart of the perfect freedom of God. He never has need to change His mind!

We begin to see this when, as psychologists, we think about freedom in connection with a human will. As long as we persist in thinking that free will has anything to do with unmotived actions, the ability to do this or that just as we like, we get into hopeless confusions. As Dr. Hadfield points out in Chapter IX. of his admirable "Psychology and Morals" the "will is the self in action." As far as the self is organized, as far as the whole organized self moves deliberately, because that self is what that self is, the action is free. So far as the self is unorganized, so far as it is pulled this way or that by some inclination or passion, so long as there is "war in its members," so far as any action is not the outcome of the deliberate movement of the whole self, just so far that action is not free. The organizing of our self, the winning of our freedom is precisely what we are here to begin to achieve. The freer the man, the more you can count upon what he will do. The freer the man, the more uniform, within the limits of his powers, will be his conduct. Freedom and consistency go together.

Only one Man on this earth achieved His freedom, and certainly one most striking thing about that perfect human life was its entire consistency. We speak of God *Himself*, using of God the word "*self*" as we use the word "*personality*," that is, recognising that both terms, as we have experience of them, must be quite inadequate. So far, however, as we can allow ourselves to think of God's *Self*, we must think of His as a Perfect Self, a Perfectly Organized Self. The Universe that Science has revealed to us—a real Universe, a rational Universe, a Universe of law and uniformities—is the only sort of Universe that could be the work and could express the mind of One, Who because He is a Perfect Self, has in Him "no variableness or shadow caused by turning."

The moment that we let every orderly sequence and uniformity in the world—etheric, electrical, magnetic, gravitational, expansive—reveal the Presence of God, the Mind of God, the Energy of God, we begin to obliterate imaginary lines between what is sacred and what is profane, and to welcome every fresh item of knowledge about the world. The more we learn of its secrets, the more consistently it bears witness to the revealed character of God. Only with this new outlook, which was impossible for our forefathers, can we recover what I have called *their general position* of thinking in the same sort of way about God and the world. This kept them free from many of our intellectual perplexities. It also enabled them to enjoy a religion which was never dull because it never lost its sense of reality.

V.

Not only is the sort of world which science has revealed to us, the only sort of world that could bear witness to a God Who is perfectly free and Who, therefore, has no need to change His mind and to rectify mistakes; but clearly it is the only sort of world in which progressive life could win its way to self-consciousness and personal freedom. As Professor Simpson says:—"The conception of natural law gives us our basis of understanding the world, as also in great measure the World-Ground. In the aspect of uniformity it represents for us the idea of self-consistency, almost what a Scriptural writer describes as a "faithful," *i.e.*, trustworthy, Creator. Without that similarity, or measure of regularity and dependableness, we could have had neither science nor theology, and experience would have meant nothing. It is only in a largely settled order of things that spirits could develope in the knowledge and love of a God." *

If the purpose of this world was that we might settle down comfortably in it, it would be a very ill-constructed affair; but it is the most ingeniously constructed world imaginable if, once more to use M. Bergson's words, the object of human life is "to accomplish, by a kind of miracle, the creation of self by itself." Determinate uniformity of the proximate environment is one necessary condition of the winning of freedom. It is only because God (so we must suppose) has limited His freedom, that there can be any indeterminateness in His world. With life there does come in an element of indeterminateness, and as

* "Landmarks in the Struggle between Science and Religion," page 161.

life progressively developes towards self-conscious persons, the element of indeterminateness, unforeseeableness, grows larger and larger. It can only be the Self-limitation of His own freedom by God that makes this possible. Only when human wills align themselves with God's will, do they restore to Him His freedom. They do so align themselves in prayer. Herein lies one of prayer's deep secrets.

Probably with no part of our religion is there more need for some readjusting of our thinkings than with regard to prayer. Popular ideas about prayer, like popular ideas about God, are ingrainedly Old Testament. They have, of course, been handed down to us by generations, whose conception of Biblical inspiration forbade any idea of development. They regarded Old Testament and New Testament alike as parts of a static revelation. For them was impossible the way in which we quite easily and naturally regard the Old Testament as containing a history of God's gradual revelation of Himself to man. For us a chief interest is the way in which very crude ideas about God are by prophet after prophet cleared and cleansed, till the notion of a tribal God, a God Who repents, Who changes His mind, Who can be coaxed or pacified, is sublimated in the idea of One, Holy, Infinite and Eternal.

But just as it was easier for our forefathers to see evidences of God in special happenings in what they conceived as "a static multiverse" than it is for some of us to hear Him speaking in the orderly regularities of our dynamic universe; so prayer to a Being Who is open to persuasion, to persuasion even to change His mind, is a simpler thing for thought than prayer to God Whose perfect freedom lies, not in changeableness but in perfect Self-determination. What room is there left for prayer, if we regard any idea of persuading God to change His mind as an absurdity? The answer is, of course, the same as the answer to the question previously suggested—"What room is there for the freedom of God where we see nothing but orderly uniformity, a reign of law?" "All the room in the world." Only, of course, we must think of prayer and all its effectiveness as being wholly inside, indeed itself a part of, the will of God Himself. Co-operation, not persuasion, is the aim and end of prayer.

Much Science now finds the ultimate of all things in Infinite Energy; some Science would add consciousness as well; presently all Science must reach Infinite Conscious Energy and will, as the Ultimate, then re-write the first verses of S. John's Gospel in modern terms. The whole inorganic world is an expression of energy, can be resolved into energy. Living things are something more than an expression of energy, for "they exhibit a directive control over energy, which leads to its further availability." When we come to Self-Conscious Persons, they are certainly more than expressions of energy; they are something more than directive controllers of energy; they seem to have been themselves entrusted with a portion of that Infinite Energy which Science finds to be the ultimate of the world. Anyone can supplement and re-write this sentence in religious language.

VI.

The moment that we think of prayer in terms of energy, most of its intellectual perplexities vanish, and we can hardly miss the conviction that prayer is and must be just the most effective outcome of energy and direction of energy in the world. As trustees of an individualized portion of the World-Energy, we can use it, if we will, against the will of God; certainly we can use it in ways that make us in no sense co-operators with Him; or we can of set purpose put it forth in conscious union with God Himself. This is what we do when we pray. In the chapter called "*Jesus' View of the Universe*" in his *Landmarks in the Struggle between Science and Religion** Professor Simpson writes "On any view of the Person of Jesus, the supreme and constant place that prayer had in His life is peculiarly noteworthy. And it is just here, in this recognition of the fundamental value of prayer as a means of correspondence and co-operation with the mind and will of God, and of setting man in new and determining relations to God, that it is possible to test the truth of Jesus' method."

---

* This whole chapter is so admirable and illuminating that it is worth anyone's while to get hold of it and read it, even if they cannot manage the whole book.

No better illustration, perhaps, of what may reasonably be thought to happen on a great scale when we pray, could be found in what seems to happen on a small scale when we think, for instance, that we will go for a walk. Within our physical organism are stores of unstable substances, which, like gunpowder, need only a spark to explode them, food-stuffs—carbohydrates and fats. A considerable sum of potential energy, accumulated in them, is ready to be converted into movement. These stores of energy have been gradually and slowly borrowed from the sun by plants, and have been assimilated by us as food; they represent one of nature's great processes on our behalf. Plants, as Bergson picturesquely says, fabricate explosives; animals fire them off. When we think that we will go for a walk, our thought seems to use our brain like a trigger and off we go, with our muscles moved for us by the exploding of hundreds of thousands of quick firing guns! Our thought was the direction of a tiny modicum of energy. Its effectiveness lay in the releasing of some of the accumulated potential energy in our organism.

When we pray the only sort of prayer that can, happily for us, be effective—that is, prayer in accordance with God's good will, or, in other words, "in the Name of Christ"—we release the energy of God in a world in which God's good will is of necessity limited by the very freedom that He has put us here to win. Go back for a moment to the Call to Prayer to which I have referred. We believe that it is God's will that all men shall be saved and come to the knowledge of the truth. Here is our guarantee for stored up unlimited potential energy. God waits for us to release it. If He released it without waiting, the very purpose of this world would be defeated. Because, in accordance with His purposing, we are free persons-in-the-making, God waits for us to put forth the hair-trigger energy of prayer.

If Christian people, in response to the present call, will thus use at least some part of the energy with which they are entrusted, we may look for vast results along lines which at least fit in with what we are more and more coming to believe about God and His world. How the stored up energies of God's will can be released by our prayer, it would be foolish to speculate. Our Lord has taught us to speak confidently to the Eternal Father. How the divine energies of God's good will, released by our prayer, can take effect we cannot even guess. We know hardly more, however, as to how our thought energy releases the stored-up energy in our bodies for physical movement. We think, and things happen; let us pray and there will happen things much greater still. Real prayer is a putting forth of energy. That is why it is so difficult. *Orare* really is *laborare*, to repeat an oft repeated phrase. Sloth is a deadly sin. It, more than anything else, kills prayer.

This conception of prayer as the putting forth of energy to release vaster energies of God, fits in very convincingly with a great deal of Our Lord's teaching about prayer. Faith is the chief thought-energy of man. That is why it so often flags if we get ill, and why sick people often find it so difficult to say their prayers. They have not got the energy. It is upon the praying person's faith rather than upon any persuadableness of God, that Our Lord lays stress always. God's good will He takes for granted. Faith which is like a grain of mustard seed and, like a grain of mustard seed, grows; faith which cancels the future and anticipates God's gifts; faith which will go on and on putting forth its energy—it is on this that the effectiveness of prayer is made to depend. This is why persistence in prayer is requisite. Little prayer means little out-put energy; much prayer, much energy. This is why quantity as well as quality matters in the case of prayer. Ten people can put forth more energy than one. When ten people agree together to pray for this or that, they are really doing something. The energy of prayer is as real a factor in the world as any other form of energy—*e.g.*, as the energy represented by electricity. Perhaps one should say that it is the same energy, only entrusted to persons-in-the-making and being used by them in the most rational and effective way.*

Once we begin to think about the world, and about God and consequently about prayer, *in the same sort of way*, it seems to me that another consequence

* See Note at the end of this Chapter.

follows concerning the world to come. We must begin to think about this in the same sort of way too.

I have already quoted once or twice from Bergson's *Mind Energy* and I close my introduction with a paragraph from the same book :—"Let us confess our ignorance, but let us not resign ourselves to the belief that we can never know. If there be a beyond for conscious beings, I cannot see why we should not discover the means to explore it. Nothing which concerns man is likely to conceal itself deliberately from the eyes of man. Sometimes, moreover, the information we imagine to be far off, even infinitely distant, is at our side, waiting only till it pleases us to notice it.

Recollect what has happened in regard to another beyond, that of ultra planetary space. Auguste Comte declared the chemical composition of the heavenly bodies to be for ever unknowable by us. A few years later the spectroscope was invented, and to-day we know better, than if we had gone there, what the stars are made of."*

Some people prefer to leap to conclusions rather than to plod first over the heavy ground which is their way of approach. If the reader is one of these, he had better turn at once to chapters III. and IV., *Through Christian Telescopes* and *Along the Curve* and come back afterwards, if he wants to, to chapters

* "Mind-Energy," page 28.

I. and II. *The World we live in*, and *Organic Evolution's Mental Concomitant*. There is no reason why one should not take the conclusions first and the reasons afterwards and some may find the conclusions more interesting and easier reading than the reasons.

NOTE.

* Thinking about prayer in this way, I seem to have no difficulties over praying about a thing like the weather—no intellectual difficulties, I mean. I may hesitate on the ground that I do not know what really is best. But the weather, whatever it may be, is an expression of energy. With it the energy expressing itself as electrical has, I believe, much to do. How one thing acts upon another, I do not pretend to know. Perhaps no-one knows. But I can see no sort of reason why the sort of energy that I, with others, may put forth in prayer should not, if it be within the will of GOD, affect the weather as much as electricity or any other form of energy in the world. When we pray "according to His will," we restore to GOD for His use the energy He has entrusted to us and which, because we are only in process of winning perfect freedom in His service, we can use either with Him or against Him. I have personally no doubt that when a group of persons set themselves to pray for the recovery of someone who is sick, their own thought energy, directed GOD-wards, becomes itself through Him healing energy contributory to any recovery that may result.

The World we live in.

I.

"I saw also the Lord sitting upon a throne, high and lifted up, and his train filled the temple. Above it stood the seraphim; each one had six wings; with twain he covered his face; with twain he covered his feet, and with twain he did fly. And one cried unto another and said, Holy, Holy, Holy, is the Lord of hosts; the whole earth is full of His glory." A wonderful vision of a wonderful prophet of long ago. *

* * * * *

"Perhaps even the most 'profane person' has some secret shrine where he allows himself at least to *wonder*. What may not the object of this wonder be—the grandeur of the star-strewn sky, the mystery of the mountains, the sea eternally new, the way of the eagle in the air, the meanest flower that blows, the look in a child's eyes? Somewhere, sometime, somehow, everyone confesses, 'This is too wonderful for me.' The sense of wonder varies in expression according to race and temperament, according to health and habits, according to the degree of culture and freedom. But whatever be its particular expression, the sense of wonder is one of the saving

---

* Isaiah vi., 1—3.

graces of life, and he who is without it, might as well be dead. It lies at the roots of both science and philosophy, and it has been in all ages one of the footstools of religion. When it dies, one of the lights of life goes out."*

* * * * *

"The revelation of order and of power as of the very essence of the world process, the recognition of something akin to reason rather than to caprice as operative at the core of things . . . must profoundly influence not merely man's highest thought and deepest feeling, but every endeavour that is made to increase the sum of human knowledge. Under this conception of the religious temper in Science would fall to be included that sense of wonder, even of reverence that is strong in the heart of every scientific man whose eyes are really open . . . . As he reflects upon the evolutionary outlook with its vast perspective of progressive achievement, he is filled with a sense of wonder which surely is not far removed from the worship 'in spirit and in truth.' 'He that wonders shall reign, and he that reigns shall rest.' Nor shall his rest be troubled by any apparently humbling discovery even in the natural history of man; for he will have realised that the whole process is of God."†

So write the two prophets of modern science, to whose books I have already referred and shall be

---

* "The Bible of Nature," J. Arthur Thomson, page 3.

† "Spiritual Interpretation of Nature," J. Y. Simpson, page 51.

making frequent reference. Like Isaiah they have seen a vision. He saw it in a moment in the Temple at Jerusalem; they, through long years of study in the temple of the Universe. Their utterances are typical. Science itself during the first quarter of this century, has been growing its six seraphs' wings before our eyes. We can hardly miss the meaning of Isaiah's picture. With twain they covered their faces;—*Reverence;* with twain they covered their feet—*Humility;* with twain they did fly—*Activity*. How vast are the fields open and opening to knowledge; how little we really know; how limited are our faculties for knowing—such thoughts are to be found *passim* in the works of the greater scientific men of to-day. And we must be dull indeed if we cannot see seraph-wings of activity as we note with admiration untiring and unapplauded labours to discover remedies for man's worst ills, and the courage and self-sacrifice of medical missionaries and others to carry the beneficent results all over the world. Sometimes, too, the ether waves that Science has learnt to direct and handle, bring us as we sit and listen to our wireless, the voice of Science itself, repeating in its own language something very like the hymn which one cried unto another;—"Holy, Holy, Holy is the Lord of hosts: heaven and earth is full of His glory." If the posts of our doors never move and if we never see or smell the incense, it can only be because that we ourselves are so exceeding dull.

II.

The vastness of the Universe—immensities of space; immensities of time; the minuteness of its exquisite perfections; the very figures mean nothing to us; but we do know that it is vast with a vastness and minute with a minuteness of which our fathers never dreamed. Through our telescopes we see stars as they were two thousand years ago since when the light has been travelling to our little earth at the rate of 186,000 miles a second. Man's time of residence on our little earth, we have to reckon in hundreds of thousands of years, and the long processes which made it habitable for him, in millions. "Our little earth"—tiny, rather, as compared with literally innumerable other great worlds among which it is the merest speck.

No wonder the thought sometimes rises in Christian minds—is it credible? Is it credible that to so insignificant a corner of so stupendous a whole, "He by Whom all things were made, for us men and for our salvation came down from heaven and was made Man"?

Now I have never been able to feel satisfied with the answer that to be impressed by size is a mere trick of our imagination; that you cannot weigh beauty or measure goodness with a footrule; that in contrast with the worlds we call mental, moral, and spiritual, the physical universe is as nothing. I think that the immensity of the Universe not only is tremendously impressive, but that it ought to be impressive. I think that it ought to compel us to revise many of our thinkings. I have already quoted a statement that our traditional theology rests on an astronomy which we have not believed in for two hundred years. Is it an overstatement that "the thought of the average man is not even Copernican; it is crudely Ptolemaic"?

When the earth was thought to have been created in a week and to be the centre of the Universe, with sun and moon and stars arranged about it to give it heat and light, it was not unreasonable to suppose that the whole might be scrapped another day by the *fiat* of the Almighty and be replaced by something better for those to live in who survived the grave. But I do not see how we can think like this about the Universe as we know it to-day. *This must be, surely, the only Universe that is or is ever going to be;* we are in it and shall continue to be in it through eternity, if through eternity we continue to exist. Science seems to suggest that at some distant date the earth may exhaust its stores of heat and become uninhabitable by man or indeed by any other sort of physical organism. If, like the author of the second Epistle of S. Peter, "we look for a new earth" and for the new heaven about it, our outlook cannot be called unscientific. I hope myself that there will be a new earth and that I may get my turn upon it and leave it, not by death, but by something like our Lord's Transfiguration. But the new earth will still be part of the old Universe—at least we have no sort of evidence to the contrary.

There are those, I know, who conceive that the world to come will have nothing to do with either space or time. Of spaceless and timeless existence I find myself unable to form any conception whatever. A future existence that will know nothing of either leaves me quite cold. I do know that I am living in a quite overwhelmingly great Universe, and it seems to me that our wisdom is to think our thoughts inside it. I expect that when we try to think outside it, we think nonsense.

Giving, however, full value (if I may so phrase it) to the immensity and, to say the least, probable permanence of the Universe, the comparatively insignificant dimensions of the earth need not cause us a moment's qualm about the central doctrine of our Christian faith. Minute as it is in the Universe, the earth may well be an item of paramount importance to the whole. Indeed if we are Christians, we must, I think, assume that it is so. Something must be going on in this workshop of the earth, which can be done nowhere else, and something on which depends the achievement of nothing less than the purpose of the Universe itself.

Two illustrations have always helped me. A motor car is a veritable Universe compared with one of its sparking-plugs. It does not surprise us if its chauffeur, or the owner himself if he is his own chauffeur, takes any amount of pains and time, if need be, to get a sparking-plug right if it goes wrong, tiny thing as it is in the great car. The universe of the car, so to speak, will not go without it. My own conviction is that something is being done on the earth of such vital importance in the Universe and for the Universe, that when something did go wrong here, the Maker of the Worlds did Himself come down to put it right.

My other illustration is from a Pottery. I remember years ago being shown round one of the great works at Etruria by the Managing Director himself. We saw process after process, culminating in ware of exquisite design and workmanship. In the middle of our walk round, my guide was fetched to a dirty little corner of the great works where sundry vats stood nearly full of semi-liquid clay. To these my guide himself added first a little of this and then a little of that. Other folks then gave the whole a stir and the material was ready to pass on for further processes. But what went on in that dirty little corner of the Works was essential to the output of the whole. Had anything gone wrong there, there it would have had to be put right—there at all costs, for the whole product of that Universe of Works depended upon it.

As a sparking-plug to the motor, as the mixing-room to the Pottery, so is the earth to the Universe, at least that is how I see it. Our Christian faith "is, let us boldly avow it" as Bishop Westcott says, "an amazing faith." But it is not unreasonable. It concerns the way in which the Author Himself put right, and put right where it had gone wrong, something upon which depend the working and the welfare of the Universe itself. The greater the immensity of the Universe, the more reasonable our faith—our faith that, even at an infinite cost, an essential part was saved for the sake of the whole.

III.

What, then, is this business of so great importance to the Universe which is going on on our little earth? What is the purpose of the factory, as I have elsewhere called it? Elsewhere, too, I have answered the question in words quoted from Mr. McDowall's "*Evolution and Atonement*";—"If we see purpose in the world at all, it is for the development of personality that the world came into existence."*

Assuming, then, that the world has a purpose, and assuming that its purpose is the development of personality; assuming, too, (as I think we must if we are to talk sense) that a purpose involves a Purposer and that such Purposer cannot Himself be less than Self-conscious, if what He designs issues in self-conscious persons, what--if one may venture so to speculate—must have been the fundamental problem? I can only think of it as the problem how—to use a figure—a drop from the ocean of the World-Consciousness could gradually and permanently be separated from the Ocean, how a particle of the Whole could achieve such compact individuation that it might return whence it originated without being reabsorbed.

---

* "A Soul in the Making," page 39.

It has been said by a great Scientist, and I daresay it is true, that to-day we know more about spirit than we know about matter, which itself seems to be just one aspect or condition of energy. At least we know that, when we contrast spirit, or mind, or consciousness with matter, it is matter that separates, that brings division and precision. Our bodies separate us one from another. But for our bodies, two of us could sit on the same chair. One aspect, at least, of what we call the material world is its existence as an instrument of division. "Thought is a continuity, and in all continuity there is confusion. For a thought to become distinct, there must be dispersion in words. Our only way of taking count of what we have in mind is to set down on a sheet of paper, side by side, terms which in our thinking interpenetrate. Just in this way does matter distinguish, separate, resolve into individualities, and finally into personalities, tendencies before confused in the original impulse of life."

It was rather a shock to me when I first read this passage in M. Bergson's "*Mind Energy*," as till then I thought I was going to be the first person to put it just like that. Put just like that, it seems to me to make the whole thing clear. Here we are in a material world, with our inherited instrument which, while it enables us to get and keep in touch with our physical environment, limits us in every direction. Only under these limiting conditions, or at any rate best under these limiting conditions, can we do what we are here to do—begin to create a self. That portion (as one must describe it) of the Conscious Energy of the World, with which we are entrusted, must here and now begin that process of individuation the result of which may be and is meant to be a self-conscious person with eternal value. I use the word *eternal* and not merely the word *survival*. What I mean by it is value for and in the Universe with all the spaciousness of the Universe. Our earth life is very limited; limited both as to time and space and by the narrow limits of our faculties. Such limitation is the very condition of the process of individuation which should issue in a being capable of a life—a life as large in comparison with our life here, as the Universe is incomparably larger than the minute portion of itself that we call the Earth.

To suppose that there are no other beings in the Universe than human beings, seems to me to be ridiculous. Probably there are beings innumerable and much greater than we. If they have achieved individual self-conscious personality, I find myself obliged to suppose that somewhere and somewhen they too have passed and have passed successfully through some process of individuation under conditions akin if not similar to those of our own earth life. *

* In his "The Problem of the Future Life," Dr. A. H. McNeile surmises that there *may* be personalities which have never been in the body. Certainly there may be and probably there are many who have never been in a human body on this earth. But I cannot help thinking that any and every sort of created personality must have been individuated by some process similar to, if not the same as, that through which we are struggling here and now.

Life as we know it on this earth needs much to justify it; for the faith that is in us as Christians we need to be able to show good reason. If there is no other way or if there is no simpler or better way in which self-conscious beings can come into existence; if such self-conscious beings can here and now begin to achieve eternal and infinite value, the end does justify to reason and to conscience the sweat and turmoil of the means. "Heirs of God and joint heirs with Christ," we listen to the words, sometimes without much thought. But they are stupendous words. We shall be "joint heirs" when but not until we can move as freely and familiarly in the Universe as we move in our own home.

"Be of good cheer, I have conquered the Universe."—ἐγὼ νενίκηκα τὸν κόσμον. So is majestically summed up the achievement of a perfect human life. That the Church should have chosen as one of her great descriptive titles the epithet Catholic, was surely prophetic. The epithet is sometimes used to describe very little things; but it means, as great as the Universe. Our fathers thought as largely as they could in the cosy little world of their conception of it. We cannot justify the use of the same great title of ourselves to-day unless we begin to adjust our thinkings to the immensities to which we are introduced by the knowledge of what has, perhaps rightly, been called "man's adolescence." The best Catholic perhaps is he who is beginning to feel most at home in the Universe.

The theory that this earth life of ours is a sort of factory process; that spirit can only be individuated by being plunged, so to speak, into matter; that to become a self-conscious person a particle of the Conscious Energy of the Universe must be embodied, is at least suggestive as regards any life of a world to come. If a person is to be permanent, it seems at least unlikely that he will ever be able to dispense altogether with what was the very condition of his becoming a person at all. Perhaps "a disembodied personal spirit" is a sort of contradiction in terms. This does not, of course, necessitate just the same sort of physical body as that which we inherit for use here. Some less limiting and limited instrument for self-expression may be appropriate for a person, no longer in-the-making, but made. But something corresponding to the body which renders possible the making seems likely to be requisite for the permanence of the finished product hereafter. Absence from the Creed of any article concerning the resurrection of the body might sorely puzzle a Christian biologist. Its presence, *pace* some modernists, is what he would naturally expect.

IV.

The chief business of our Earth Factory is the making of persons. With this view of its purpose, all that we cover by the large word Evolution, broadly interpreted, is consonant. A large theory to begin with, the theory of Evolution has itself been going through a process of evolution since Darwin wrote his epoch-making book, "*The Origin of Species*," in the middle of the last century. "For those who have lived all their days," writes Professor Simpson, "in an age whose Open Sesame has been "Evolution," it is not easy to realize the tremendous revolution in thought that followed the publication of Darwin's work entitled *On the Origin of Species by means of Natural Selection and the Preservation of Favoured Races in the struggle for Life (1859)*. The modern difficulty indeed, is, to understand how it was ever possible to entertain any other ideas about the origin of species than those that in general obtain to-day."*

A great deal which Darwin, with the wisdom of great learning, tentatively suggested, has since had to be modified and much, which more dogmatic followers have from time to time asserted, has failed to stand the test of fuller investigation. No-one is to-day, I imagine, satisfied by any theory of accidental variation as a principal factor, or perhaps as a factor at all, and few hold that any theory of natural selection can account for even a considerable part of the whole vast evolution of Creation. "Natural Selection is," as Archbishop D'Arcy says, "a sifting process and a fixing process. It is nothing more. All that is really creative must be presupposed before its process begins." To-day indeed we all recognise that "it is not the survival of the fit that calls for

* "Spiritual Interpretation of Nature," page 122.

remark. What excites our interest is the question *not of their survival but of their arrival;* it is the question of the origin of that fitness itself, for there is no wonder in the survival of that which is fit to survive."

Admitting, however, all this, it is safe to assume that most people take for granted that our world of things and organisms, as we know it to-day, came into being by a process "of continuous, orderly, broadly progressive change, from the simple to the more complex, which arises as the resultant of various factors, operating from within and from without. Typically we see it in all embryonic development, that marvellous process by which a fertilised egg-cell grows by segmentation and concomitant differentiation into an organism of its own species. In the development of the hen from a microscopic germ-cell, through the intermediate stage of the chick into the adult, we have an instance of continuous, orderly, and broadly progressive change, from the simple to the more complex, which arises as the resultant of various factors operating from within and from without."*

As we look at the whole process, it is easy to see that it has been a movement towards increasing fullness and more abundance of life. Our forefathers thought that the Universe was geocentric, that the great whole centred round the earth. To-day science

* "Spiritual Interpretation of Nature," page 108.

is replacing the word *geocentric* by the word *biocentric*. Only as interpreted in terms of life can any meaning be given to the whole. It took the earth, so to speak, hundreds of millions of years to reach the stage at which organic life upon it became possible, and life has been unfolding and achieving its possibilities for more millions of years ever since.

During our life-time Biology, the science of life, has filled, not books, or shelves, but libraries. Life is still the great mystery. None-the-less about life on this earth of ours we do know a great deal. If when we speak of "the life of the world to come" we mean at all by the word "life" *there* what we mean by the word "life" *here*, then the Biology of this world simply must have something to tell us about the Biology of the next, if not in the details, at least in the great outstanding features of that age-long development which began with an amoeba and has reached self-consciousness in man.

I say *age-long development*, for this is the proper subject of biology. What lies behind the age-long development is not within her scientific purview. Her business is to teach us to think about the world, not merely in terms of chemistry and mechanics, but in terms of life. She is proving to be for our generation an admirable teacher. To teach us to think of *life* in terms of *God* is the proper business of Theology—to teach us *to think in terms of God of the ordinary and every-day life of the world we know*, of the sort of life with regard to which biology has so vastly increased our knowledge. When she does so Theology will regain her throne as Scientia Scientiarum. "For most thinking men in these days the ultimate question often is, What kind of a world am I living in? Yet modern theology has been little enough interested to make them feel and see that the world in which they find themselves is God's world, and so they remain dissatisfied or indifferent, or content to leave theology as an amiable diversion for minds of leisure. There is no challenging resounding argument from the age-long travail of a world which has issued in man, and which, by the pervading purposiveness of its process and the proved potentialities in man, hints both at the character of its Ground and the further possibilities of the individual human life." *

I think that this is a true bill. Just as it still seems possible to take a high medical degree with next to no acquaintance with psychology, so it seems still to be possible to get a first in Theology at a great University with no knowledge whatever of natural science. "The invisible things of Him from the creation of the world are clearly seen, being understood by the things that are made," so wrote S. Paul. To-day the elaboration of this text is being left too much to the Scientists by the Theologians, with some loss to Science and ruinous loss to Theology.

From the conviction that the Universe is bio-centric to the conviction that the Universe is Theo-centric

* "Man and the Attainment of Immortality," page 7.

is no great step. Of this fact the opening verses of S. John's Gospel are a standing reminder. Indeed we think perhaps most truly when we regard Theology as just an older way of spelling Biology. Certainly they are twins, if not one science, and each has continual need of the other. Almost every problem of biology has its theological aspect and *vice versa*. That this is true of the Atonement itself, I have tried briefly to show in my *A Soul in the Making* (pp. 63-73) where I wrote "any theory of the Atonement which makes it less than a cosmic happening is inadequate for our biological need." I will not repeat here what I said there. But it is as a biologist (as far as I may call myself one) that I should see nothing but a *cul de sac* before the human race, did I not believe that He by Whom the worlds were made has Himself hewed for mankind a way back into the main stream of life, out of which it had turned *by sin* on the level of self-consciousness as irrevocably as * all forms of life below him in the evolutionary process had done before him *by error*.

V.

If not in its details, certainly in some of its outstanding features, the biology of this world must have something to tell us about the biology of the world to come. If *life there* means something totally different from *life here*, we ought not to call it life at all but something else. So we go on to note three

* But see page 113.

or four characteristics of life here, purposing afterwards to extrapolate forward the curve of our this-world biological knowledge.

(a)

The main-spring of all organic progress has been some sense of need in the organism and some effort on the part of the organism to satisfy it. "A sense of need issuing in some fresh act of trusting self-committal has been the main-spring of all organic progress, mental and material and without these there had been no experience, no fuller and more abundant life." Life probably began in the water. Had none of those elementary water-organisms wanted somehow to wriggle through the mud to life on dry land, we should all be fishes still. We owe these primæval heroes a great debt. I believe that something like a million years is computed as the period taken by countless organisms, by efforts and experiments innumerable, to convert water breathing by gills into air breathing by lungs. I sit here breathing comfortably as I write, inheritor of the fruits of heroic efforts. The eye with which I watch my page began as just a spot sensitive to light in some very humble brother of long ago. Had he not wanted and had he made no effort of active response to the light, I should not have the admirable instrument with which I see to-day. I wonder how many elementary heroes tumbled into the water and got drowned in making their invaluable optical experiments!

Of course I do not mean to suggest that the organism's own effort was by itself creative. I do suggest, however, that it was essential to the gradual realization of something which, but for the effort, must have remained potential and ineffective. How we are to interpret what looks like behaviour in the very humblest organisms, their experimental efforts to secure food or to escape from foes, is a question of very great interest, but we are not specially concerned with it here. The point that I want to make here is that some striving to satisfy some desire has always and everywhere lain behind life's progress. No effort, no progress, seems to be a fundamental biological law.

The next point I want to make is this. "We live by faith." It may seem a far cry from the inexplicable striving of some elementary organism, with a pigment spot sensitive to light, to the faith by which I go to the station to catch a train, make plans for to-morrow, count upon my friend, or say my prayers. None the less the self-committal and reaching out towards the future and the unseen on the level of consciousness, which I call my faith, bears the same relation to my humble little ancestor's efforts of milleniums ago as my two excellent and amazingly intricate eyes bear to his or its elementary pigment spot.

Man's physical evolution has slowed down almost to stopping. By inventing tools, man himself removed the urge of need and desire. To the deer fleetness was a matter of life and death; but man learnt to ride upon horses. If with advancing years and much study your eyes begin to fail, you go and buy a new pair of spectacles. Clearly man's further evolution does not lie on the physical plane. Man's mental instrument also is probably about as polished as it is ever going to be, and wonderfully polished it is.

To the vague sort of urge and striving that seems to have been the spring of all evolution, the name "appetency" has been given. It must always have been more or less vague since it has been reaching out to an inexperienced future. Our ancient friend with the pigment spot can have only had the dimmest notion of what he wanted when some urge prompted effort to get light-wards. Perhaps this "appetency," which seems to have been the spring of progress, is best thought of as a vague sense of dissatisfaction prompting to effort.

Prompting to, but by no means necessitating effort, or the world would not consist mainly of species which have reached equilibrium and have ceased to evolve.

In man life has broken through, so to speak, into self-consciousness—the Life has become the light—and for him new realms of evolution are thereby opened up. Appetency or some widely felt sense of dissatisfaction prompting, but by no means necessitating, effort, will mark the line of his future progress. We might have guessed and, along this line of thought, we can be sure that it is with his religion that any future progress is bound up. This, of course, is why all real religion means sustained effort and why, if one is in comfortable circumstances, it is perfectly easy to reach a sort of equilibrium and get along without any religion at all. It also explains why those who reach the equilibrium of a comfortable existence are often the most dissatisfied people in the world. Religion is difficult just because it is making something. Carrying bricks to the top of a building must always be a laborious job! In the effort lies the value and the temptation to let it alone.

Those of us who have chosen the ministry of religion as our walk in life often need heartening up. That "a knowledge of history is the best cordial for drooping spirits," is a famous and true saying. I am not sure that some knowledge of science is not an even better cordial still. If everybody wanted religion and found it easy and delightful to be religious, religion would not and could not be what it is—man's true line of evolution.

Often our own drooping spirits arise from the knowledge of how difficult we ourselves find religion to be and how little of it we really have got. The gripping of reality is always an ordeal and science would suggest that our self-dissatisfaction is just the Universe's *sine qua non* of any betterment through our ministry for ourselves or for anyone else.

It is also, I think, good to recognise that the value of a Church never depends upon its delightfulness or the admirable smoothness with which it works. The value of a Church depends upon the amount of effort it can call out from its members. Sometimes, I expect, it is doing its very best work when, from the point of view of those who are not evolving, it looks least satisfactory and when, from the point of view of those who are, it seems to make overdemands upon their loyalty and patience. I always feel glad, when musing over such scraps of science as I have got hold of, that I am a member of the Church of England!

Few things in the world are so easy to criticize as hymns, especially the popular ones. No sort of hymn comes in for more apparently sound criticism than those which paint glowing pictures of life beyond the grave and of our longings to get there. Those who in this connection make use of that always most dangerous-to-the-user weapon, ridicule, show their lack of biological insight. Such hymns—some of them written centuries ago and quite magnificent, like *Jerusalem my happy home*—are valuable just because their exaggerations are suggestive and stir sub-conscious appetency. Certainly one outstanding lesson to be drawn from the whole evolutionary process of life is that no-one is in the least likely to become qualified for any next world at all, who has no wish for anything beyond this present.

If (a) the mainspring of all organic progress has been some sense of need in the organism and some effort on the part of the organism to satisfy it, organic progress itself has been continuously in the direction of (b) *freedom by means of increased faculty*, and (c) of *individuality by multiplication of relationships.*

(b)

Organic progress has been in the direction of freedom. Low down in the scale of life, the organism is almost wholly determined by its physical environment. Powerless to move or to see or to hear, it is wholly at the mercy of its surroundings. The road to freedom lies, not in the direction of getting away from the proximate environment, but of getting more and more in touch with it, by increased faculties, and with more and more of the total environment of the Universe. The transition, however it was achieved, from the condition of cold-blooded organism to that of warm-blooded organism, was a transition to greater freedom. For its temperature the cold-blooded animal is entirely dependent on the medium in which it lives. The warm-blooded animal, as it has been picturesquely said, carries its own weather about with it. It would be as easy as it would be tedious to fill pages with illustrations. The fact is that "the result of Evolution at every stage is seen to be a growing freedom from the domination of the proximate physical aspects of the environment." So writes Professor Simpson and adds:—"This develops in the case of man into a progressive control of them through growing commerce, rapport and union with the ultimate spiritual Reality in that Environment. With him, moreover, the freedom to be won covers the whole range of his animal past. Progress, Life, Evolution throughout have depended on growing adaptation to ever deeper and wider aspects of the Environment."

On two points I want to lay stress. The first has often been stressed before, but it really is decisive. Freedom has been won by growing commerce, rapport and union with environment through the development of new faculties. Once upon a time, sight, hearing, locomotion were new faculties, new freedom's factors, if you like. Development of faculty through appetency-motived effort on the part of an organism has always meant *reaction to a real environment*. Had there been no such thing as light, there could not have come into being any such instrument as an eye. Man's appetency-motived efforts have, as a matter of fact, resulted in what can only be called religious faculty, if not in all, at least quite certainly in some. Under these circumstances to doubt the reality of an Ultimate Spiritual Environment—or, to put it more shortly, God—would seem to be unscientific. Science, like experience, cannot shut its eyes to the fact that there are bound to be many who will not, perhaps cannot, make the effort necessary to grow the faculty for getting in touch with anything wider than the proximate physical environment. But that a more ultimate and real and

Spiritual Environment is, so to speak there, to be got in touch with, cannot reasonably be doubted.

The second point on which I want to lay stress is this—for further progress towards further freedom what must be needed is increase of faculty. Sir Oliver Lodge put down in a sentence a suggestive, if startling truth, when he wrote—"there is no next world, save subjectively."* The Universe, in one small corner of which we find ourselves, is large enough and varied enough and wonderful enough in all conscience. *What we need is more faculty.* Our planet is, by comparison, only a tiny atom and "on our planet there are numberless objects with which it is impossible for us to come into relation simply because of our physical constitution; and of those objects of which we are aware, it is only with some few aspects that we can become acquainted. This conception of a world beyond our senses supplies us with an arena of momentous possibilities. We lack entirely a sense for electricity, being unable to distinguish between positive and negative electricity. Were we so endowed, a new world would dawn on us and Science."† I believe that it is true to say that, if we could sense electricity, there would be for us no empty space at all!

In the direction of changing and controlling of our proximate physical environment, we have made astonishing progress. I live in an environment

---

* "The Making of Man," page 32.

† "Spiritual Interpretation of Nature," page 17.

almost wholly man-made. Man made the surface of the ground on which I walk and pretty nearly all the things I see. He fills my atmosphere full of smuts but brings me filtered water through a pipe to wash them off with. If it rains, he provides me with a macintosh and umbrella to keep it off. If anyone thinks for a minute, he will realize how astonishingly we have modified our proximate environment. The principal limitations to our freedom lie in the physical instrument through which we contact our world. We inherit it; we have little power of modifying it; it gets ill; it wears out. It looks as if completer freedom must lie for us in the direction of fuller control over the instrument through which and in which we are set here to make ourselves.

For the making of ourselves our present limitations are probably essential; they are the conditions of our material experience. I find myself obliged to conclude that they are the only possible conditions (or at any rate the best conditions) under which a particle of the Self-Conscious World Energy can be individuated. But the whole process of Evolution seems to suggest the reaching of a stage at which free control may be won by the individuated person over that most proximate environment of all—his own body. Certainly the idea of development towards ability to make for one's self the appropriate instrument wherein to function on this or any other plane or planes of the Universe is not less scientific than it is obviously attractive. It may not be what is going to happen, but it is not unlike what, looking at the whole course of the evolution of the world behind us, we may quite reasonably anticipate. We have no need or reason to hope for another world—if by world we mean Universe—except subjectively. We do need to have done with sin and sickness; to be freed from the limitations of our inherited physical instrument; to have more, any amount more of faculty. If such a prospect quickens appetency, we are wise if we read the lesson of the ages that only by effortful reaction to something wider than the proximate environment has any sort of faculty ever been made.

(c)

The organic process has been continuously in the direction of individuality by multiplication of relationships. An outstanding feature of organisms on a low level of life seems to be the exact opposite of individuality—they continually divide. A unicellular organism would be well described as a dividual. As the physical organism increases in complexity and integration, division begins to mean destruction. Some worms can, I believe, be divided segment by segment and each segment will become a new and complete worm. You cannot so treat a human leg! Corresponding to this progress towards physical individuation, the same sort of progress is observable on higher levels. In his chapter on the *Evolution of Individuality* and speaking of man, Professor Simpson says:—"In the forms of life below him, the vital emphasis apparently is laid upon the species; it is in the interests of its survival that the constituent individuals appear to lead their lives, and, as sometimes happens amongst lower forms, perish after reproduction of their kind. In the higher phases of organic evolution, not only is there a general reduction in the number of offspring, but the life of the individual is maintained long after the period of reproduction is past. It looks as if in the case of the end term of the process, the individual was coming to have a peculiar meaning and significance."

As in the case of progress towards freedom, so in the case of progress towards individuation, it would be easy to fill pages with illustrations. The particular point, however, that I want to make is this. Just as progress towards freedom has been won by increase of faculty, so more and more of individuality has been won by the multiplication and strengthening of relationships. Every step towards individuality has meant more dependence on others—a sort of combination of opposites. In his *The Ascent of Man*, Professor Henry Drummond follows his chapter on *The Struggle for Life* by a chapter on *The Struggle for the Life of Others* and in them works out, with a good deal of detail and, I think, convincingly that we get the whole idea of organic evolution wrong unless we recognise that almost from the start there have been two forces at work *pari passu*, the *Self-regarding* instinct and the *Other-regarding* instinct. "The first chapter or two of the story of Evolution may be headed the Struggle for Life; but take the book as a whole and it is not a tale of battle. It is a Love story." The progress of life has been made possible by the increasing care of offspring by parents and by the give and take of mutual helpfulness in colony or herd.

In just the same strain Professor J. Arthur Thomson writes in his fascinating "*The Bible of Nature*" in the last section of his chapter on *The Evolution of Organisms.* I can only quote a sentence:—"Must we not recognise that progress depends on much more than a squabble around a platter; that the struggle for existence is far more than an internecine struggle at the margin of subsistence, that it includes all the multitudinous efforts for self and others between the poles of love and hunger; that self-sacrifice and love are factors in evolution as well as self-assertion and death; that existence for many an animal means the well-being of a socially-bound or kin-bound creature in a social environment; that egoism is not satisfied till it becomes altruistic." Individuation by interdependence would seem to be a law of the whole organic process.

Man is clearly much more of an individual than are the animals below him and, during infancy, he is for much longer and more completely dependent on others than they are for his very existence, while to the end of his days he is dependent on others for all his well-being. We live in an age which sets a higher value upon individual life than any preceding age has done. Closely, though not at first sight obviously, connected with this is our growing sense of the interrelatedness and interdependence of all the nations of the earth. It looks as if a growing recognition of wider and wider relationships, coupled with a deeper and deeper sense of indebtedness and obligation, must be one of the fundamental conditions of the growth of any sort of individuality that is to have survival value. Survival value is bound up with morality. *

It is tempting to add several more items to our biological curve before speculating as to where its extrapolation leads us, but by so doing I should overload it for my purpose. I must, however, before following along the direction which it seems to indicate, add some speculative considerations which to some will probably seem absurd, but which I do myself think have in them the cogency of sound sense.

---

* "It is a sure sign of shallow thinking to put individuality in man into antithesis to his corporate and social life. Tyranny, it is true, depresses individuality, but corporate life intensifies it." Bishop Gore, "The Holy Spirit and the Church," page 115.

Organic Evolution's Mental Concomitant.

I.

Let me begin this section with a paragraph from Professor Blewett's *Study of Nature and the Vision of God,* quoted by Professor J. Arthur Thomson in his *System of Animate Nature* (Vol. II., page 375). "In insisting upon the continuity of nature, men of science have been better theologians than the theologians themselves. If God exists at all He is the God of all nature and of every law. There are no gaps in His workmanship, no breaches of continuity in His activity. All nature is an activity of His, and every natural law a principle of that activity. If the theologians would be true to theology, what they have to do is to protest, not against the principle of continuity, but against too narrow a reading of it, and too narrow an application of it to reality. The principle of continuity is unworthily treated if it is limited to certain physical and chemical processes. The true field of the principle of continuity is the total history in time, the total evolution." This chapter is a sermon on this text.

Heredity is, of course, as Professor Thomson says "not so much a factor in evolution, as a condition of evolution. There would be heredity though there were no evolution, but there could be no evolution if there were not heredity." Heredity involves continuity of some sort. Science has, therefore, been at immense pains to find a basis for continuity and it has found it in the continuity of the germ-plasm. The foundation of modern embryology is the fact that the essential germinal material, from which generation after generation springs, is from generation to generation handed on intact. Back of the embryo, which developed into the great-great-grandson, is the very same material which was back of the embryo that developed into the great great grandfather. Here Science has discovered—and it is a wonderful discovery—a sure basis for continuity. No wonder Science has been tempted to attribute to the germ-plasm more than it is, I venture to think, conceivable that the germ-plasm can carry.

A germ-cell is, of course, not an ordinary cell, though an ordinary cell is utterly overwhelming in its wonderfulness. A germ-cell is, perhaps, the most wonderful thing in the world. Science may well attribute to it all that can be put into language, as long as the words retain any meaning. When, however, it is described as "a condensed implicit individuality," or as "a psycho-physical being telescoped down"; or when I read that "a complete inheritance, rich in initiatives, endowed with the gains of past ages, may be condensed into a microscopic egg-cell and in a sperm cell 100,000 times smaller," I find myself wondering whether language is not really beginning to disguise incompatibilities. It may be that Science is at present obliged to put it in this way. Science sees continuity and development everywhere but finds no sure basis of continuity anywhere except in the germ-plasm. Therefore to the germ-plasm must be attributed evolution's whole inheritance, including what can only be described as *inherited experience*.

Writing of the earliest organisms, Prof. Simpson says "they must have lived before a fund of heritable organic experience was collected," but, for later stages, the passing on of what is best described as "heritable organic experience" is assumed. I am not sure that the Professor may not have felt the same sort of perplexity that I feel over such a phrase as the telescoping down of *experience* into a cell, for, speaking of a germ-cell, he writes *"across this infinitesimal vital viaduct passes the condensed experience of millions of individuals."* * Nothing could serve me better than this delightful figure to make clear the point I want to make. That which passes over a viaduct, be the viaduct large or small, *is never part of the viaduct itself* I doubt if what happens could be better put and I could wish for no better description of what I believe myself to be, than, one for whom the condensed experience of millions of individuals has passed over the infinitesimal vital viaduct of a fertilised germ-cell, produced through the

* "Spiritual Interpretation of Nature," page 313.

long travail of a world,—a germ-cell, which has developed into the physical instrument which I call my body—my body, in which I may and ought to create a self with eternal value in the Universe. But I do not believe that the condensed experience was ever *in the germ-cell* or that words describing it as having ever been in the germ-cell, potentially or otherwise, really have any meaning.

II.

I want next to ask two questions—(1) Can there be experience without an experiencer? To this question there is, I think, only one answer—No. By the word experience we mean something that is experienced by something that has some sort of consciousness. If we speak of the experience of a piece of iron, we are using the word figuratively.

If, then, there cannot be experience without an experiencer, (2) can experience, condensed or uncondensed, be transmitted *without a continuing experiencer?* I think that Science was perfectly right when, seeing that physical continuity and development was a fundamental principle of the organic process of the world, she concluded that there must be some physical *continuum*, and proceeded to look for it. She looked, and with extraordinary patience and skill, found it in germ-plasm. But evolution clearly involves much more than physical continuity and development. It involves mental continuity and development, it involves *transmitted experience.* Is it not reasonable to conclude that there must be some conscious *continuum* through the ages, to account for this order of facts, just as Science concluded that there must be some physical *continuum* to account for another order of facts and concluded also that when modifications of a permanent sort arise in this or that organism, such modifications in the organism must have begun as modifications in the germ-plasm?

For a great many years it has seemed to me that we simply must make room in our thinkings for some invisible and conscious concomitant of physical development, if we are to have a rational theory of organic evolution and the conclusions of the two Professors, from whose works I am continually quoting, serve to strengthen the conviction. Both, when they come to ultimates find that they cannot stop short of two. Both seem to suggest that the two ultimates may be resolved into a higher Unity, but that such resolution cannot be deduced from scientific evidence. Thus towards the end of the first volume of his *System of Animate Nature*, (page 344), Professor Thomson writes:—"The general outcome of the present discussion is an appreciation not only of the pervasiveness of mentality in the realm of organisms, but of all penetrating purpose as well. Looking back imaginatively on the course of evolution, we have seen the emergence of an aspect of reality which we call Life, and another aspect of reality which we call Mind, now we are getting glimpses of another aspect of reality which we call Purpose." On the next page he continues:—"At this stage it seems as if part of that purpose were the emergence of individuality, mind, freedom, purpose. This thrilling word purpose, expressing the most real fact of our personal experience, brings us at this half-way house to our provisional conclusion which is, we confess, too large for the premises, that individualities with mind, with freedom, and with purpose, cannot be accounted for in terms of a ground of reality without mind, without freedom, without purpose."

In slightly different words, towards the end of his *The Spiritual Interpretation of Nature* (pages 269 and 270) Professor Simpson reaches very much the same conclusion. "On the views that have been enunciated in the preceding pages," he writes, "it would appear that we are left with Consciousness and Infinite Energy as two ultimates; we may even venture to think of the former as the informing spirit of the latter," adding on the next page, "Of such an ultimate in consciousness viewed as the informing spirit of energy, we may conceive the progressive manifestation through instruments of increasing organization and complexity, each better adapted for partial revelation and expression, till finally in man is produced an individuality that is able to come into direct relationship with the Ultimate in its most personal aspect."

Two ultimates—Life and Mind or Infinite Energy and Consciousness—two ultimates of the process of organic evolution. If we have to think of them as *two* at the start, is it not reasonable to think of their progressive manifestation as *two-fold* during the process? Science has been keeping its eye on the process's "instruments of increasing organization and complexity"; perhaps it was bound to keep its eye on them. But in the long process that seems to eventuate in individuality, is not something more involved than "instruments of increasing organization and complexity," is there not involved the progressive individuation of that which is manifesting itself through the instruments? I think that there is.

It would be difficult to find a more illuminating description of what is meant by *The Word* in the first verse of S. John's Gospel than Professor Simpson's phrase "Consciousness viewed as the informing spirit of energy." The two ultimates of the world-process find their unity in a Person. The world-process itself eventuates in persons, and in each person once more Consciousness and Energy find their unity. A person is a being entrusted with a particle of the Conscious Energy of the Universe. But in the long process leading to the creation of self-conscious persons, at least for purposes of thought, we do well to distinguish two lines of development—the development of Energy in the shape of "instruments of increasing organization and complexity" and the concomitant development or individuation of the consciousness which is using the instruments. A process which began from a Unity and ends in unities is best viewed as two-fold in its unfolding. Some such view of the process alone makes it possible, as it seems to me, to give meaning to such necessary biological phrases as "condensed and heritable organic experience."

III.

When, by thinking of my own experience, I try to give understandable content to the phrase "condensed experience" I am conscious of two ways in which my own experience becomes condensed, so to speak, for me. It becomes condensed into instinct or into faculty.

In the days of my youth I was taught to make a reverence towards an Altar in a Church. I have done this so long and so often that the action has become instinctive. I am apt to do it without thinking and not to do it would mean conscious effort. Experience has been condensed into instinct. I sit here and type off this page at a great rate, scarcely troubling to look at the keys. I got my first typewriter thirty-five years ago. Experience has been condensed into faculty. Of course the instinct is mine and the faculty is mine because the experiences have been mine—the *experiencer* has continued. I myself have been my own *continuum*.

As I look at the organic process of the world, I seem to see everywhere evidence of the development of just these two things—instinct and faculty. In the only case that I can test, they have meant a mental *continuum*. It seems to me reasonable to conclude that in the world process they have meant some mental *continuum* also.

It would be delightful to fill a page or two with instances of altogether wonderful instinct. Anyone who has not read Sir John Lubbock's *The Senses of Animals* and Lord Avebury's *Ants, Bees and Wasps* will find them delightful reading. For precise, recurring, organised and co-operative action there seems to be nothing in the world to touch instinct. Yesterday I asked a brother parson what he made of a hive of bees—where lay, so to speak, the mentality through which, on the loss of a queen bee, a worker bee, by the co-operative efforts of the hive, in an enlarged cell and with special feeding, was transformed into a new queen. He thought it was in the antennae; but I don't think he had thought about it at all. Such highly organised and co-operative action means—unless the book of Nature is deceiving us—long experience and long experience must mean, I think, a long continuing experiencer.

I find it impossible to escape from the conviction that behind and expressing itself through a hive of bees is some abiding group-mentality. Generations of bees rapidly come and go; they seem to express a mental *continuum*. Such mental *continuum* is not, I imagine, much affected by the coming and going of the generations through which it expresses itself. It is dependent upon them as the instruments of its expression, and the more highly organised the instruments, the fuller the expression of its condensed experience. But it does not die with the death of the bee. Year after year a generation of Painted Lady butterflies appears and disappears. The life expressed through it does not cease with the fragile and beautiful instruments of its expression. It re-incarnates next year.

Highly organised instincts and the highly developed organisms, through which they function, must, I imagine, have a long history behind them both, and it certainly does look as though, in the development of the Arthropods, part of the Ground Consciousness of the world has taken a direction wherein development, reaching perfection, has come to a full stop. The road of instinct does not look like one of life's thoroughfares.

The road of faculty is the thoroughfare along which life has broken through to self-consciousness in man, and along it, in process of individuation, has moved the World Consciousness, finding in the animal world "instruments of increasing organization and complexity" for its expression. In the higher animals there is still much of instinct, but coupled with it, more and more of faculty and intelligence. An intelligent dog is rich in both faculty and instinct. Both are condensed experience and both witness to some continuous experiencer. Here, again, I find it impossible to escape from the conviction that behind and expressing itself through each great animal species is some abiding group mentality, enregistering and handing on the group experience.

It may be only fancy, but I can't help fancying that somehow the hens of to-day are born with more instinct or faculty for getting out of the way of a motor car than was the case twenty years ago! If they are so born, the domestic fowl reveals one of the world's secrets.

In the case of the animals, too, as in the case of the bees and butterflies, I imagine that the life expressing itself through them does not cease when the animal dies. When a man shoots a partridge, he destroys life's admirably organized instrument; I do not think he touches the life itself.

Thinking of the whole process of organic evolution, Darwin wrote:—"There is a grandeur in this view of life, with its several powers having been originally breathed by the Creator into a few forms or into one, and that while this planet has gone cycling on, according to the fixed law of gravity, from so simple a beginning endless forms most beautiful and most wonderful have been and are being evolved." There is grandeur in it; but it seems to me that it is only one half of the story. The other half has to do with Organic Evolution's Invisible Concomitant—the World Consciousness in process of that individuation which issues at last in individual self-conscious man.

IV.

"Do you mean to say," I may be fairly asked, "that you think that organic evolution has come on its long journey by a world process of continual re-incarnation; that what you call Organic Evolution's Mental Concomitant, or the Experiencer which makes condensed experience possible, has been down the ages progressively expressing itself through instruments of increasing organization and complexity, working out in the process its own individuations?"

Yes; that is what I do think, and I think it on the same sort of grounds as those on which some physicists believe there must be an ether of space. The facts cannot be explained without it. I do not think it is possible to explain the facts of the age-long process, which is finding its climax in self-conscious persons, unless we include in our thinkings a gradually individuating spiritual concomitant, which makes the registering, condensing and inheriting of experience possible, and whose continuity is not broken by the death and disappearance of the instruments in which it gains its experience and through which it expresses itself.

Sir Oliver Lodge heads the second chapter of his book *Ether and Reality* with the paragraph: —

Apollonius of Tyana is said to have asked the Brahmins of what they supposed the Cosmos to be composed. "Of the five elements," was the reply.

"How can there be a fifth," demanded Apollonius, "beside water and air and earth and fire?"

"There is the Ether," replied the Brahmin, "which we must regard as the element of which the Gods are made."

Whatever we may think of the last sentence, it is undeniable that, by its own methods, our Western Science, or at least some outstanding Scientists, have reached a conclusion which, by entirely different methods, Eastern Thought had reached centuries ago.

Western Science does not and is not likely to entertain views of the ether of space identical with those for which Eastern Thought makes congenial room. But there was much more in what the Easterns held than, for a long while, Western Science would allow itself even to consider. The same is, I believe, true of the theory covered by the terrorizing word Reincarnation. Like other supposedly terrible things it needs to be looked at steadily. It reaches us with all sorts of Theosophical incumbrances in the shape of Eastern speculations in ill-fitting Western clothes. But the theory itself deserves to be seriously pondered and is interesting, if for nothing else, at least for the fact that it has been and still is the accepted theory of more than half mankind.

For us, of course, it is a biological question just as for us the ether of space is a physical question. Does the wonderful process, which reveals itself to us as biologists, require for its explanation *a conscious continuum* as well as a *physical continuum?* If it shows us "instruments of increasing organization and complexity" does it suggest, at any rate, some sort of mentality embodied in the instruments and itself, becoming more and more individuated? It seems to me that it does. That is why I quoted as the text of this chapter Prof. Blewitt's statement that "protest is needed, not against the principle of continuity, but against too narrow a reading of it and against too narrow an application of it to reality. The principle of continuity is unworthily treated if it is limited to certain physical and chemical processes. The true field of continuity is the total history in time, the total evolution." Continuity of Individuating Consciousness, through manifold and transitory expressions of itself, is, I believe, Life's central secret—the explanation of the whole process up to date. It will continue to be life's open secret in the world to come.

V.

I have already quoted words of Professor J. Arthur Thomson regarding the purpose of the world-process —"the emergence of individuality, mind, freedom, purpose" and words of Professor Simpson:—"till finally in man is produced an individuality that is able to come into direct relationship with the Ultimate in its most personal aspect; and words of Mr. McDowall —"If we see purpose in the world at all, it is for the development of personality that the world came into existence." Let us assume that all three are right.

Further, I am going to assume that there is at least something to be said for the theory of some spiritual *continuum* gradually making for individuation throughout the whole world process.

Clearly, if in the earlier stages of the process the spiritual individuating *continuum* expresses itself through a group—*e.g.*, a hive of bees or a species of animal—a point must be reached at which, not the group, but the individual, begins to be the unit of expression. This point is the advent of self-consciousness. Whether this point is reached by any of the higher animals, it is, I suppose, impossible to say; it is certainly reached by man. Wherever it occurs, "the appearance of personality in animality marks the introduction of a new era."

Is it reasonable to conclude that such of life's methods as are revealed by the age-long process, prior to the advent of self-consciousness, have been continued in connection with the evolution of man himself? It is, I think, not only reasonable but inevitable. We come into the world with highly organized bodies; we bring with us from somewhere highly organized faculties also. We do not doubt that our highly organized body is the outcome of the travail of a world; I see no reason to doubt that our highly organized faculties represent the condensed experience of a conscious world too. If in faculty we differ from one another, if *qua* faculty we show individuality, then I think that there is no escaping from the conclusion that we are the inheritors of some condensed individual experience.

How much should be attributed to environment and how much to the inherited mental equipment or potentiality of an infant, it is impossible to say. But I shrewdly suspect that if I had had exactly the same environment as that of William Ewart Gladstone, I should neither have got a double first at Oxford in the same year or been Prime Minister of England. It looks to me as if the bundle of faculties, which was his, was very different from the bundle of faculties which is mine, and certainly such a highly organised mentality, as was his, must have had behind it some long history—a long and, in all probability I think, individual history. If this is true in his case, it is of course true in all. For each of us "across the infinitesimal vital viaduct" of a fertilised egg-cell has passed or is passing the experience of millions of individuals and among them the experience of many souls-in-the-making which did not create selves with survival value. They did not accomplish, perhaps they could not accomplish, with survival value "that creation of a self by itself," which M. Bergson describes as "the very object of human life."

But what they did and perhaps suffered was not wasted—nothing in the world is wasted—the faculties with which I am making a self to-day are my precious inheritance of their condensed experiences. That what I have inherited has cost so much may well be a motive not willingly to prove a failure in my task to-day.

In the second essay in his book *Mind Energy*, dealing with the relations of *The Soul and the Body*, M. Bergson writes:—"The work of the brain is to the whole of conscious life what the movements of the conductor's baton are to the orchestral symphony. As the symphony overflows the movements which scan it, so the mental life overflows the cerebral life. But the brain—precisely because it extracts from the mental life whatever it has that may be played in movement, whatever is materializable—precisely because it constitutes thus the point of insertion of mind in matter—secures at every moment the adaptation of the mind to circumstances, continually keeping the mind in touch with realities. The brain is then, strictly speaking, neither an organ of thought nor of feeling nor of consciousness; but it keeps consciousness, feeling and thought tensely strained on life, and consequently makes them capable of efficacious action. Let us say, if you will, that the brain is the organ of attention to life."

All this, I think, is true and viewed thus, our brain is not the instrument which enables us to remember, but, rather, the instrument which obliges us to forget. Any remembrance of the experiences, which have somehow become condensed into our faculties, would hinder and perhaps make impossible the business of our present life—to make a self with survival value. It is at least a pleasant speculation that if we do make a self with survival value, when that self is released from the limitations of its present physical instrument, we may remember and possess the whole of the experience of the age-long process wherein He, in Whom was life, has become the Light of all our being.

VI.

Very few of us, who have grown up with the traditional outlook of Christianity to immortality, have, I think, ever really faced the new problem presented by the modern belief, not to say knowledge, that man has been living on this earth for a quarter of a million years at least. During that immense period of time, he has himself been evolving and, with him, his environment. In the case of all organisms Professor Simpson points out that "we are almost compelled to consider the organism and its environment as a single system undergoing change."* This is pre-eminently true of man. Man to-day "in commerce with to-day's active environment," must be very different from man of a hundred thousand years ago. Has each one of these countless millions, in all stages of development, been a newly created and immortal soul? If so, where do we conceive them to be and what is the meaning, if any, of this age-long process?

Our mediæval forefathers did not have any such problem to face or any hesitation about holding that

* "Spiritual Interpretation of Nature," page 101.

those, who had failed during the few thousand years of this world's school of probation, were reserved somewhere for an eternity of woe. We do not and cannot think like this.

In the chapter on *Evolution as the Winning of Freedom*, in *Man and the Attainment of Immortality* (page 261) after speaking of the transformation that results and has resulted for men of all races and civilization from direct relation to our Lord Jesus Christ, Professor Simpson hazards a suggestion, startling at first sight and incomplete (in my rash judgment) in one direction, which does, I believe, glimpse the truth. I do not hesitate to make one more long quotation as it seems to me to contain a very great contribution to our thought about these things, a contribution which is, I believe, Professor Simpson's very own.

"Throughout the world," he writes, "there is an increasing race of men—the word is not too strong, although the characteristics are not physical but spiritual—who by an act of will, bringing themselves into relation with Him, attain to yet greater liberty and begin to develop a quality of life which, if His words are true, is eternal. Accordingly, then, we may really see a double movement in human evolution, which goes deeper than the superficial siftings of nationality. The one concerns those individuals and masses of individuals whose evolution will end, like other lines of previous evolutionary history, in an *impasse*, just because the individual is at once cause and effect, without spiritual relationship, and a prey to a disrupting disharmony of mind; the other, a new line which tends towards increasing self-mastery, freedom and inward harmony. The former line will long persist, enriching civilization and itself evolving to some extent, but with no ultimate future beyond that of the limits of terrestrial existence, except in so far as its members come to realise their true destiny; it constitutes a divergent evolutionary branch. The other branch is in the true line of continued evolution."

Two phrases in the above paragraphs seem to me to suggest a wider hope—*the individual is at once cause and effect* and *except as they come to realise their true destiny.*

To my way of thinking they suggest more than a wider hope; they suggest a reasonable expectation. During the earlier stages of organic evolution the Conscious Energy of the World expresses itself through "instruments of increasing organization and complexity." The end of the process is the creation of self-conscious persons. Somewhere in the course of the process, it seems to me, (just where, so to speak, self-consciousness begins), *the Conscious Energy of the world not merely expresses itself through, but entrusts part of itself to its most highly developed instruments*—they begin to be individuals, they begin to be (to use Professor Simpson's phrase) *their own cause and effect.* They are literally part of the World-Energy individuated, and share in the indestructibility of Energy.

Whether, as such, they accomplish, "as by a miracle, the making of a self by a self" in the true line of evolution, is another matter. Many selves, created through the experiences of a human life, can have no survival value whatever, and those, whose selves they are, must be classed with the failures to achieve this world's final product in the true evolutionary line. But the whole of that with which they were furnished for the making of a self, enriched, or it may be damaged, by one more life's experience, may not unreasonably be thought to abide, for the making of a more successful soul. Once more "the condensed experience of millions of individuals" will pass over the infinitesimal vital viaduct, with the raw materials out of which to make a self and the faculties wherewith to make the same. "The true line of evolution," as Professor Simpson calls it, goes forward and my own immense hope is that when the final product reaches the world to come, it may ultimately, if not immediately, possess in memory and for ever the whole vast experience, from amœba (if you like) to S. Paul's ἄνδρα τέλειον, or perfectly evolved man, "joint-heir with Christ" and with the Universe as his inheritance.

What I mean by a Self or Soul I have tried to make clear in my *A Soul in the Making.* I mean *that bundle of feelings, thinkings, sayings and doings which is my very own.* When from my own self I strip away all that I have been given and am being given, and try to see the naked self of my own creating, I become aware (as I imagine that all who do the same must become aware) that it is a very poor thing. When I bless God for my "creation, preservation and all the blessings of this life" I can wholeheartedly add "but above all for Thine inestimable love in the redemption of the world by our Lord Jesus Christ, for the means of grace and for the hope of glory." Knowing the self that I have made, it is as a Christian and not as a biologist that I embrace and hold fast the blessed hope of everlasting life, for the particular self that I call "I" to-day. The gospel does, I believe, make possible the otherwise impossible, but it is as the divine completion of organic evolution, and not as something apart from organic evolution, that I welcome and prize it.

VII.

If anyone likes to call the outlook on the evolutionary process that I have outlined, Re-incarnation, I have no objection, so long as they do not muddle it up with any transmigration of souls theory. As a matter of fact, I do not think that what I mean by a soul or self is ever re-incarnated prior to such re-incarnation as is looked for by the article of our creed concerning "the resurrection of the body." If a self creates itself with no survival value, it can no more survive than can an organism see which has not made an eye. All that can survive for another time is the total which it received but did not create—a total enriched by its experiences condensed into more faculty, to help towards the making of another self another day—another self which may, indeed I believe will, hereafter find itself heir to something much larger than a single life on this earth.

Some readers may be inclined to think that in this last paragraph I am doing myself just what I venture to say that others do when they speak of a complete inheritance, endowed with the gains of past ages being condensed into an egg-cell, namely, using words without meaning. But I seem to myself to have inherited a mental something, over and above what can have been telescoped into the wonderful egg-cell, which has grown into my physical instrument. Call this mental something a bundle of faculties, if you like, only think of it as an organized mentality.

It seems to me that the whole psychological direction, towards which Freud and Jung have turned our thinkings, involves "a sub-conscious" which has had a long history—a sub-conscious which we did not create ourselves but which we inherited. In his *The Problem of the Future Life*, Dr. A. H. McNeile turns down the whole idea of re-incarnation in a couple of paragraphs. But a page or two further on, when dealing with Spiritualism, and in particular with Mediums and Telepathy, he hazards the question:—"Can impressions be handed on in the unconscious mind by heredity, as various other psychic characteristics probably can?" "If so," he adds, "a medium might re-act to the unconscious knowledge of a sitter, and reproduce things that were consciously known only to a previous generation." With the right answer to the question I am not concerned. All I want to point out is that both the question, and the sentence following it, assume some continuity between the conscious mind of A in one generation with the unconscious mind of B in the next. Personally I think that what was knowledge in the conscious mind of A is more likely to be in the subconscious mind of B as faculty than as recoverable knowledge; but I entirely agree with Dr. McNeile that there is continuity, if that is his view.

Indeed I find myself entirely in agreement with him in all that he says about Spiritualism.

As a field for scientific investigation it may prove to be much more fruitful another day than it seems to me to have proved to be up to the present. What purport to be messages from beyond seem so consistently to reflect the thoughts of the living, as indeed they have done at every age in which Spiritualism has become popular. Science has learnt how to turn electrical vibrations into vibrations of something else that we can sense. Some day it may find out how to render thought vibrations cognizable by us also. This is not likely to be achieved with less scientific experiment and knowledge than that to which we owe our wireless.

To regard Spiritism as a sort of new popular religion seems to me to be something worse than ridiculous; and that for the unscientific medium it is horribly dangerous must be patent to anyone who knows anything about it. For most of us communion with those who have gone on before is much more likely to be satisfying and wholesome on the mountain top of prayerful thought than in the stuffy cellar of some amateur séance. Personally, as I have not time to pursue spiritistic investigations scientifically, I let them alone. If others, with the necessary time and scientific training, make fresh discoveries, I shall be among the grateful oncs. I can see no sort of impropriety about such investigations if they are properly conducted and with a view to scientific knowledge, by which I mean, as I have said before, "Knowledge *with the personal factor eliminated*"—which, of course, in the amateur séance, it never is.

Of messages purporting to have come from friends departed, those have always seemed to me the most interesting which, at first hearing, seem almost ridiculous. I mean messages which describe experiences in the world to come as immediately and exactly like experiences here. Most people who take any interest in spiritistic matters will remember the description of things beyond given, as was believed by those who received it, by a young officer killed in the war. Included was something very like a war-time canteen.

But if we pass on from this world, not so much with a ready-made spiritual body as with the capacity for making one hereafter, it seems likely that many will find themselves to begin with in a sort of dream world. If we survive at all, in some sort of dream world we must be confined unless or until we have some sort of body-instrument wherewith to come in contact with the realities of any future world. If, under these conditions, any of us find it possible to send messages, such messages will be dream messages and reflect our experiences in the last places we were in during our earth life. A message purporting to be from a young officer and describing something like a canteen seems to me to bear on its surface evidence of being veridical—a real dream message. Such messages could obviously have no value for fresh knowledge and would be likely to be very inconsequent.

From such evidence as we have, I get the impression that it may be possible for those, who have quite recently died and have hardly, as it were, got away, to transmit their thoughts; but that, when they get or begin to get a body with which they can contact some of the realities of the world to come, they either find it much more difficult or are themselves much less inclined to communicate what they know.

These last paragraphs are a parenthesis here; but I shall want to refer to the same subject in my last chapter on Expecto.

Through Christian Telescopes.

I.

Now we can get out our Christian telescopes through which to follow the direction of our curve, for through Christian telescopes we shall have to look if we are to see it going on at all. Non-Christian Biology holds out little hope, if any, of eternal life for man. It is quite right. Only because the inevitable has been avoided and the impossible has been achieved can man go forward.

I have already quoted the best description I know of a law of Nature:—"A generalised statement, a conceptual shorthand report of Nature's observed uniformities of action." On these uniformities being uniformities and invariable, the whole Universe depends. As Professor Simpson says—"Just as a varying multiplication table would be the destruction of mathematics, so would a varying law of Nature be the destruction of the Universe." Not in the department of mathematics, but *in the sphere of life* a law of Nature has been reversed. The Universe has not been destroyed, because the Maker of the Universe reversed the law Himself, in His own Person and at infinite cost. This is the meaning of Calvary.

A law of life has been reversed for man—the simple but foundation law of the whole of organic evolution that there can be no retrogression. Whatever direction an organism or group of organisms takes, in that direction it must go on. If it once turns out of the main stream of life, leaves the direct but narrow path of upward evolution, it cannot go back. Had it been able to do so, the whole process would have been thrown into confusion. Everything below man in the scale of life has as a matter of fact at some time or other turned out of the main stream and left the narrow upwards path *by error* * and nothing can go back and start again. In man Life has broken through into self-consciousness. On the level of self-consciousness, Man has *by sin* done exactly what everything before him did by error—he has left the path of upward evolution. This is the scientific truth underlying all that Christianity calls the Fall. A man must be completely ignorant of himself if he cannot see that the old picture in Genesis is a picture of himself, even if it is a picture of no one else.

Nor do I think that to regard evil, as we know it in our world, as merely failure, is adequate to experience. Failure evokes or ought to evoke sympathy and help and nothing else. But there are forms of evil which evoke repulsion and disgust. Sins of cruelty, lust, meanness, treachery are of this character. About them there is something positive and horrid. We seem here to be up against something different in character from mere difficulty or inertia calling out

---

* But see page 113.

wholesome effort. I doubt if S. Paul was far wrong when he described our wrestling as being "against the principalities, against the powers, against the world rulers of this darkness, against the spiritual hosts of wickedness in the heavenly places." We seem to be up against an evil will. That is why I think that to describe evil negatively and as failure is inadequate to experience.

In spite, however, of obvious failure and, it may be, of something worse, man can get back into the main stream, because a way has been hewn back into it for him; man *can* pick up again the line of upward evolution, because on his behalf the law of no retrogression—no going back to start again,—has been cancelled, and he can repent, Calvary was a cosmic happening. This point is for my whole argument so important that I venture to quote one paragraph from my *A Soul in the Making*.

"For man's salvation nothing less was needed first of all, than the cancelling of a fundamental law of the whole evolutionary process itself by which life has reached self-consciousness in man—the law of no retrogression. Something cosmic had to happen. Life must negate part of the method devised by itself for its own expression. From exactly such a cosmic happening Christianity sprang—*Life died.* We may not be able to explain or comprehend; but if man's need calls for nothing less than the reversal in his case of a law of life's evolutionary process, here at any rate is the utmost cosmic reversal that we can conceive—Life did its exact opposite and died, and death did its exact opposite and opened the road for further evolution. No wonder the light of the sun was blotted out! Was there ever such a paradox. 'But to take this paradox out of Christianity, is to make it shallow and superficial beyond recognition.' " * Through Christian telescopes the way is open for the extrapolation of our curve.

There is of course nothing new about this way of putting things as witness some of the magnificent old hymns that we sing at Passiontide year by year to the puzzlement of members of our congregations who have lost the cosmic point of view.

"God in pity saw man fallen,
  Shamed and sunk in misery,
When he fell on death by tasting
  Fruit of the forbidden tree;
Then another tree was chosen
  Which the world from death should free.

Therefore when the appointed fulness
  Of the holy time was come,
He was sent Who maketh all things
  Forth from God's eternal home;
Thus He came to earth, incarnate,
  Offspring of a maiden's womb.

---

* "The Idea of the Holy," page 11, Rudolf Otto.

He endured the nails, the spitting,
Vinegar and spear and reed;
From the holy body broken
Blood and water forth proceed:
Earth and stars and sky and ocean
By that flood from stain are freed.

So wrote Bishop Venantius Fortunatus in the last half of the sixth century, before men had let their religion become less Catholic in its outlook than the Universe in which they conceived themselves to live.

II.

With my naked natural eye, unaided by my Christian telescope, I see in front, not the extrapolation of a great curve, but a vicious circle. By sin man has turned again and again out of the narrow upwards path leading to freedom and true individuality—leading to the creation of a self by himself with eternal value. An endless round of self-created selves without survival value is all that the naked natural eye can foresee, if it sees clearly—an endless round until the particle of individuated cosmic energy, with which they were entrusted, is re-absorbed into the ocean of Cosmic Energy—Nirvana—from which it came.

I am too old to respond to the World Call to the Church by any offer of service abroad. If, however, I found myself a missionary to the East, what I should want to say to my Buddhist friends would be, not that what they seem to believe about the future life is untrue, but that it seems to me to be so horribly true. It is the truth of man's hopeless plight apart from Christ. What we tell people in sermons, is quite true, scientifically true; man cannot right himself. To be saved from this plight is what I mean by Christian salvation. News that this hopeless round need not be our fate, is the good news of the Gospel of Jesus Christ. What I should want to say would be—What brings me to India is the fact that what so many of you believe is so true and is so wretched, and from it I believe that I know the only way through Jesus Christ our Lord.

Like Re-incarnation, Karma is a word which needs to be looked at steadily. It means just that from which Christ came to set us free. As S. Paul says—"The law of the Spirit of life in Christ Jesus made me free from the law of sin and death." (Rom. viii., 2). "Sin is lawlessness" (I. John, iii., 4). If you sin against a law of nature—the law of gravity, for instance—penalty follows as effect follows cause. Rigid incidence of law (of cause and effect, if you like) in the Spiritual sphere is Karma. No one has warned us more solemnly or directly than Our Lord Himself of the fatal incidence of Karma on those who, by unforgivingness, put themselves outside of the pale of salvation. He calls it 'prison.' "Verily I say unto thee Thou shalt by no means come out thence till thou hast paid the last farthing" (S. Matt., v., 26). If you would learn by contrast what is meant by Salvation, think out Karma and be thankful.

Eastern intuition arrived at the existence of an ether long before the slower methods of our Western Physical Science discovered it. By the same sort of intuition the Eastern mind has forestalled by centuries our Western Biology which is still more or less unwilling even to look seriously at what is perhaps the oldest and most widely held doctrine concerning man's future. Western Biology will never see in any theory of re-incarnation and karma what Eastern Intuition has accepted and what Western Theosophy has somewhat crudely embellished gilding the chains thereof. But Western Biology will find it really does clothe a truth regarding the *impasse* from which Christianity claims to offer a way of escape. How indeed shall we escape, if we neglect so great salvation—escape from Karma?

If this whole section startles some of my readers and to others seems absurd, I would ask them, before they turn it down, to try to get clear for themselves what they really do believe about the future of those who, through their own fault or not through their own fault, are quite definitely not in Christ.

Some few, but it will be very few, may suppose that such are reserved for eternal punishment.

Many will have to admit that they are hoping that somehow everything will come out all right for everybody in the end—of which most popular and most demoralising Creed Professor Simpson truly says: "Nothing so robs life of its tremendous seriousness and meaning, reducing it to the level of a marionette show, and belittling man's fateful capacity to choose life or death, as the amiable outlook of Universalism." It need hardly be said that by no stretch of imagination can it be identified with the outlook of Christianity.

Most might have to confess that they had never given anything worth calling thought to the problem at all. In weighing up any theory, it is always well to face the alternatives. I see no alternative less incompatible with Christianity or more congruous with Biology than that which I have outlined in this section. To any reader, who does not agree, I would say, what is your alternative?

III.

We have looked, so to speak, through one of the two lenses of our Christian telescope, for there must be a second. There is nothing dynamic about the cancelling of a law and what the plight of man clearly needed and needs is more dynamic. That to help him with the making of a unified self, Christianity provides him with the pull of a realized personal ideal, I have dwelt on at some length in my *A Soul in the Making*. But man needs more even than the pull of a realised personal ideal, be it ever so strong and attractive, if he is to get back to his true line of evolution and stick to it when he has got there. Circumstances proved too strong for him before and they will prove too strong for him again. I see therefore a second biological need, if the purpose of the whole world process is not to end in failure.

A need is not in itself evidence of a supply. But if something is clearly needed for the fulfilment of what appears to be a great purpose of a great Purposer, the expectation that the need will be supplied is reasonable. This quite obvious need Christianity claims to have found in the gift of the Holy Spirit. "The Spirit was not yet given, because Jesus was not yet glorified" (S. John vii., 39).* To interpret this subjectively, making it equivalent to a statement that the disciples were not yet capable recipients, has always seemed to me quite superficial and to argue some blindness as to what is man's real need. What man needs is more power from on high and power *in a shape that he can assimilate and use*. This is the gift of His own Spirit by the Ascended Christ—human and divine.

Man seems to live between two mediators—one of the physical and one of the spiritual world. He has no power of assimilating the mineral world. As mediator between him and it is the vegetable world, which can take in carbon di-oxide and other such things and turn them into food-stuffs for the animals and for man at the head of them. Man can neither eat minerals nor can he see God's face and live. But

* Dr. Weymouth translates the Greek exactly "for the Spirit was not yet, because JESUS had not yet been glorified." This only strengthens my point.

he can see "the light of the knowledge of the glory of God in the face of Jesus Christ (II. Cor., iv., 6).

In a passage of singular beauty and suggestiveness, Bishop Gore in his Essay on *The Holy Spirit and Inspiration* in *Lux Mundi* (pages 320-321) traces the history of man's failure to assimilate and to respond to the Divine Spirit and adds:—"In Christ humanity is perfect and complete, in ungrudging and unimpaired obedience to the movement of the Divine Spirit, Whose creation it was, Whose organ it gave itself to be. The Spirit anoints Him; the Spirit drives Him into the wilderness; the Spirit gives Him the law of His mission; in the power of the Spirit He works His miracles; in the Holy Spirit He lifts up the voice of human thankfulness to the Divine Father; in the Spirit He offers Himself without spot to God; in the power of the Spirit He is raised from the dead . . . . . . Christ is the second Adam, who having 'recapitulated the long development of humanity into Himself,' taken it up into Himself, that is, and healed its wounds and fructified its barrenness, gives it a fresh start by a new birth from Him. The Spirit, coming forth at Pentecost out of His uplifted manhood, as from a glorious fountain of new life, perpetuates all its richness, its power, its fulness in the organised society which He prepared and built for the Spirit's habitation."

Man needs, if he is to regain and to keep in the true line of his further evolution, something more than increased receptivity, he needs a new sort of gift. The Holy Spirit sent to us in Christ's Name is "*the Spirit of Jesus.*" "This is a title," says Bishop Westcott, "to be pondered. We rightly shrink from endeavouring to define Divine relations by human language. Yet as we feel the vital importance of the truth which the Western Church desires to guard by affirming the procession of the Spirit from the Father and the Son, we feel no less surely that relatively to us the activity of the Spirit proceeding "from the Son," for Whom the Incarnation is not potential only but realised, Who has taken up into Himself, as He is seated on the right hand of the Father, the fulness of humanity *is other than it was*, to use the language of time, *before He came down on earth*. After the Ascension the gift of the Spirit, as the Spirit of "Jesus the Son of God" Who has passed through the heavens, *is different, not only in degree, but in kind* from that which was before, separating by the whole breadth of human life the Old from the New,*

On pages 302 and 303 of his *The Holy Spirit in the New Testament* Dr. Swete says "The Spirit of Jesus, the Spirit of Christ is also described as the Spirit of the Son of God. *God sent forth the Spirit of His Son into your hearts*. The Son is here the Incarnate Son . . . . The Spirit is expressly and repeatedly associated with the glorified life of our Lord in

---

* "The Incarnation and Common Life," page 114.
See also Bishop Gore, "The Holy Spirit and the Church," page 114.

heaven . . . . . . The Spirit was not in the world in the fuller sense until Jesus was glorified . . . . *The Spirit which* God has *made to dwell in us* is the Spirit of the glorified Lord."

Could I imagine myself as a biologist coming across Christianity for the first time, I think that its doctrine of the Cross and of the gift of the Holy Spirit would grip me at once. Any thinkings I might have had about some possible life in some possible world to come, would have been brought up short by the obvious fact that man has turned out of his true line of evolution and is by a fundamental law of the whole process barred from getting back to it and by the further fact that, even if he could get back, the same conditions which caused his failure before would certainly cause it again. If, so thinking, I heard for the first time the Nicene Creed, I should stand amazed. For here embedded in this old formula of the Catholic Church are met, and scientifically met, my two scientific needs. He by Whom all things were made, Himself cancelled the prohibiting law and from Him, with the Eternal Father, comes forth the Holy Ghost the Life Giver. Man can rejoin his true evolutionary line, with power from on high, in a shape which he can assimilate, to abide in it.

IV.

"And was incarnate by the Holy Ghost of the Virgin Mary." Again, if I could imagine myself hearing these words for the first time as a biologist,

I should, on second thoughts perhaps, be filled with the same sort of amazement. The central doctrine of Christianity is not of course that the most wonderful of men was born and that in him dwelt more fully than in anyone before or since the Spirit of God. The central doctrine of Christianity is that *The Word*—the Conscious Spirit informing the Energy of the Universe—"was made flesh and dwelt among us" with "the glory of the only begotten of the Father full of grace and truth."

My first thought might be that this story of a Virgin Birth was an unnecessary miracle invented to embellish a great happening. But on second thoughts, and thinking as a biologist, I should have to pause. A germ-cell is not an ordinary cell. As I have said at some length above I do not myself think that there can be "condensed" or "telescoped" into it all that it is sometimes made to carry. *But it does represent a certain definite line of inheritance.* A fertilised germ-cell represents two such definite lines coalescing. If we had sufficient knowledge, a microscope might, I imagine, show us the two lines of inheritance ramifying back through the centuries. But they would be *two definite lines.* Over the infinitesimal vital viaduct (once again to use Professor Simpson's figure), passes no doubt the experience of millions of individuals, but it is the experience of a quite limited part of the organic world. From it normally can develope no more, in the shape of a human being, than an inheritor of that large but *limited* condensed experience. If He by Whom all things were made, gathering up the experience of the world itself, and not merely of two definite lines of human development, was incarnate, then it was not by a normal birth that He was born.

For the Virgin Birth the historical evidence may or may not be very strong; the scientific necessity for it is absolute—if Christianity is true.

From conversations which I have had with people, there are, I know, many who, while they feel no particular difficulty about the Virgin Birth, do not see that it matters very much or why the Catholic Church sets so much store by it. How she came to do so, I do not know. I am quite content to believe that she was guided by the Spirit of Truth. Had there been nothing about it in her Scriptures and nothing about it in her creeds, biology would have had some day and in some way to have guessed at what somehow she knew. I do not mean to say that biology would have guessed at just the form of the wonderful happening that we have received by tradition; but I do think that biology must say that, if He Who was born at Bethlehem on the first Christmas Day could cancel a law of life's organic process and can by His Spirit enable men not only to recover but to cling to the line of their true evolution, then He was not born by normal generation.

He was born of a human Mother. In his *Ascent of Man* Professor Drummond devotes a chapter to the *Evolution of a Mother*, and begins it with these two paragraphs.

"The evolution of a Mother, in spite of its half humorous, half sacriligious sound, is a serious study in biology. Even on its physical side this was the most stupendous task Evolution ever undertook. It began when the first bud burst from the first plant cell, and was only completed when the last and most elaborately wrought pinnacle of the temple of Nature crowned the animal creation."

"What was that pinnacle? There is no more instructive question in science. For the answer brings into relief one of the expression-points of Nature—one of these great teleological notes of which the natural order is so full, and of which this is by far the most impressive. Run the eye for a moment up the scale of animal life. At the bottom are the first animals, the Protozoa. The Caelenterates follow, then in mixed array the Echoniderms, Worms and Molluscs. Above these come the Fishes, then the Amphibia, then the Reptiles, then the Birds, then —what? The Mammals. *The Mothers*. There the series stops. Nature has never made anything since. Is it too much to say that the one motive of organic Nature was to make Mothers? It is at least certain that this was the chief thing she did."

Drummond wrote the chapter with quite different ideas in his mind; but when I first read it, the thought flashed into mine that there was something at least very suggestive in that, according to our Christian tradition, when He who "is before all things and in whom all things consist" was Himself made Man, He chose as the human means the crown of Nature's most consummate workmanship—our Lady.

V.

"Jesus brought to His public ministry," writes Dr. Du Bose, "a character thoroughly formed and an attitude toward life definitely and finally taken." Of those years, between the ages of twelve and thirty, during which He created, what had never been created before, a perfect human self, we have no record. But, again to quote from The Gospel in the Gospels:—"The divine recognition at His baptism is a recognition, not of what He was potentially at His birth, but of what He was and had humanly become in His life." Our records tell us something of the conditions under which and of the process by which He attained, during the years of His ministry, to the height of the spiritual and moral manhood for which He stands and, as Dr. Du Bose says, "it is not in the power of our human imagination to conceive, or of our reason to suggest, how otherwise He could have attained it."

As we watch Him, we are allowed to see a perfect human Person in the making and to note at least some results of His progress along what we may surely call man's true line of evolution.

Earlier in this book—pages 40-45—we noted certain outstanding features of the whole process of evolution.

(a) A sense of need, issuing in some fresh act of trusting self-committal has been the mainspring of all organic progress;

(b) Organic progress has throughout been continuously in the direction of (1) freedom by increased faculty and (2) of individuality by multiplication of relationships.

A sense of need issuing in acts of trusting self-committal is no bad definition of faith. A sense of need, appetency, self-committal, faith—we cannot miss them in connection with the perfect Human Life. "My meat is to do the will of Him that sent me and to finish His work." "I have a baptism to be baptized with; and how am I straightened till it be accomplished!" No wonder that as those who were nearest to Him watched Him, their thoughts shaped themselves into the prayer "Lord increase our faith." Writing of Him, Professor Simpson says:—"there appeared in Palestine One who in His person exhibited perfect manhood, and whose life was at once full of the completest internal harmony, and liberty, and independence. No other life has ever given such a sense of freedom . . . . He realised in every particular that towards which the whole evolutionary process has been evidently tending."* Conscious of

* "Man and the Attainment of Immortality," page 259.

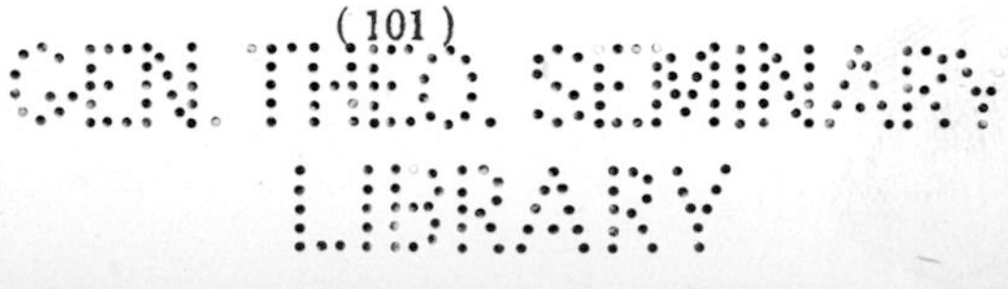

completest internal harmony through His love to God and man—of real individuality based upon the widest and closest possible relationships, He bade His followers to love God with all their hearts and their neighbours as themselves. Out of His own actual experience, He gave us, in the Beatitudes, the conditions of a happy life.

"No other life has ever given such a sense of perfect freedom" and freedom comes by increase of faculty. It is difficult to read Our Lord's life without getting the impression that He was in touch with a larger world than others. He may have been merely using the language of apocalyptic when He speaks of the Angels; but He certainly gives one the impression that He habitually and consciously moved in their company.

However this may be, it is perfectly clear, if we accept the Gospels' account of things, that by increase of faculty He had won freedom of control over His proximate environment. I say nothing here of His works of healing; what are of far more interest in our present connection are what are called the Nature Miracles. From the point of view of this book, they are exactly what might have been expected.

The whole process of evolution has been growing freedom by control of environment. Very imperfect man has a very large measure of control. In Jesus Christ we see, I believe, the sort of freedom that man would long ago have reached had he not turned out

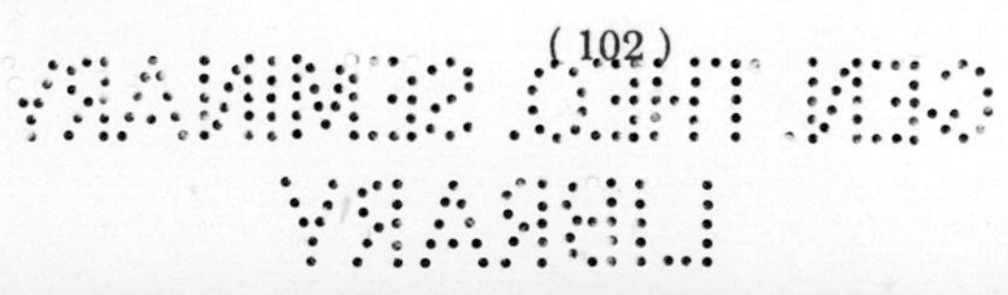

of the line of his true evolution. I feel no surprise that perfect Man fed the multitude, stilled the storm, and walked upon the sea. Had the perfect Human Person been as limited as we are with regard to faculty—that would have seemed to me to be incredible.

Nothing could be more striking than Our Lord's own attitude towards His own wonderful works; the last thing that He seems to have wanted men to think about them was that they were wonderful. Sometimes He seems surprised and disappointed that His disciples could not do the same. He did not hesitate to promise them ability, through their faith and the dispensation of His Spirit, to do still greater things—a promise that He has already begun to fulfil. The impression made by His life of "completest internal harmony, liberty and independence" has never been summed up better than by Professor Seeley in *Ecce Homo* (page 48). "It was neither for his miracles nor for the beauty of his doctrine that Christ was worshipped. Nor was it for his winning personal character, nor for the persecutions he endured, nor for his martyrdom. It was for the inimitable unity which all these things made when taken together. In other words, it was for this, that he whose power and greatness as shown in his miracles were overwhelming denied himself the use of his power, treated it as a slight thing, walked among men as though he were one of them, relieved them in distress, taught them to love each other, bore with undisturbed patience a perpetual hailstorm of calumny; and when his enemies grew fiercer, continued still to endure their attacks in silence, until petrified and bewildered with astonishment, men saw him arrested and put to death with torture, refusing steadfastly to use in his own behalf the power he conceived he held for the benefit of others. It was the combination of greatness and self-sacrifice which won their hearts, the mighty power held under a mighty control, the unspeakable condescension of the *Cross of Christ*."

VI.

The unspeakable condescension of the Cross of Christ. And the condescension was, I believe, even greater than *Ecce Homo* suggests. It was not merely that He could have avoided the Cross had He so willed; *it needed an act of will on His part, as perfectly evolved man, to be liable to death as we know it, at all.* In the Transfiguration the Perfect Man has revealed to us, I believe, what would long ago have become the way in which men would have passed on from this plane of things had they not turned out of their true line of evolution—had not sin entered in and death by sin. For a self-conscious person death, as we know it, is a horrid abnormalism—the rending of a self from its instrument of self-expression.

During the earlier and age-long stages of organic evolution the individuating Conscious Energy of the world may be thought of as expressing itself through groups and species. As I have said before, I imagine that it makes little or no difference to the life, which they express, that Painted Lady butterflies are but annuals or something less. When, however, self-consciousness is reached, when an individuated particle of the Cosmic Consciousness entrusts itself to a unit for the making of a self, it is a different matter altogether. Our Christian Scriptures consistently regard death, as we know it, as an abnormalism for man. The tendency of modern thought is to thin these things away and to interpret death in this connection as spiritual death. But there can be little doubt that when S. Paul wrote "Since by man came death by man came also the resurrection of the dead" he meant death in the ordinary meaning of that word. This ceases to be a puzzle when we begin to grasp the true line of man's evolution and how disastrous have been the results of his having left it. It is quite true that for man by man came death.

I have always thought that those who removed the Transfiguration from the red-letter days of our calendar were dreadfully prosy and lacking in imagination. They were, I believe, lacking in more; they lacked insight as to the meaning of the Transfiguration itself. To interpret it as designed to encourage three of the Apostles before the stress of the Passion or that in it our Lord allowed Himself a moment of spiritual intercourse and soul-refreshment, seems to me to be quite inadequate. Interpret it as a revelation of the normal passing on of a perfect human person, and the whole incident sheds wonderful light on all that we Christians believe to have happened afterwards. "I lay down my life," said Our Lord, "No man taketh it from Me, but I lay it down of myself. I have power to lay it down and I have power to take it again" (S. John x., 18). You and I cannot say that. It is a measure of the distance between our sinfulness and His perfection. Deliberately He willed to return to the condition brought about by man's fall that for man He might undergo His Passion. That is why, I imagine, the three Apostles were bidden to say nothing about what they had seen till the Resurrection. No wonder as they were in the way going up to Jerusalem and Jesus went before them, one of those, who were in the secret, remembered afterwards that they were amazed! On the morning of the Resurrection, our Lord stepped back to where He was on the Mountain of the Transfiguration.

To some the disappearance of the Sacred Body from the tomb is a puzzle. It seems to them an unnecessary addition. Viewed as I view things, it was not an unnecessary addition, it was inevitable. Our Lord passed on from His life on earth in what was the normal way for perfectly evolved man. He had won, as we are meant ultimately to win, complete freedom by complete control of what I called on page 54 "the most proximate environment of all," His physical body. After passing through the deliberate valley of His Passion our Lord resumed the Body of His glory (of His perfect evolution) and rose again.

NOTE TO PAGE 106.

If we hold that the Transfiguration was the Gospel's revelation regarding the normal passing on of perfectly evolved (that is, sinless) Man and that our Christian Scriptures are right in consistently representing death, as we know it, as a horrid abnormalism for man and the result of sin, we can only ponder with deepened awe and wonder the Agony in Gethsemane. For here surely we are allowed to glimpse the climax of our LORD's return to the abnormal physical condition of fallen man, which rendered Him capable of death. Gethsemane reversed for a space the Transfiguration. This accounts, as nothing else accounts, for the physical accompaniment—"His sweat became as it were great drops of blood falling down upon the ground." The ordinary physical result of mental stress, especially if it includes fear, is to contract all the vessels on the surface and to drive the blood inwards. A willed return to the physically abnormal seems to have been accompanied by an abnormal physical experience. That "there appeared unto Him an angel from heaven, strengthening Him," can help to carry our thoughts back from the deep valley of the Agony to the mountain top of the Transfiguration and on to Easter morning. In the garden we witness a chief heroic moment in the great series of heroic moments which make up the Passion.

burst any prison, and we might easily doubt whether His doing so was ground for expectancy on our part that we shall ever be able to do the same. What was demonstrated was the fact that death has no dominion over perfectly evolved man. Herein lies the joy of Easter. He Who rose on Easter Day is our Elder Brother, Who is restoring us to that true line of our evolution in which He Himself first walked and through which He won.* That He should have demonstrated to the Apostles that He had flesh and bones, that "He did eat before them" does not puzzle me at all. It is what I should have expected. During His earthly life we can see Him winning, I think, more and more freedom by control over His proximate physical environment and at last having

* If the Cross did really hew for man a way back into the main stream of life, the first gift made by the Risen CHRIST to His Apostles, through the Spirit, on the first Easter night was just what, as evolutionists, we might have hoped for. For the making of a soul or self nothing can be more important than the conviction that there has been failure, but that such failure is not final; that a fresh start is really needed and that a fresh start can be made, and over and over again if necessary; with stimulus to make it and assurance that it has been begun. The Commission to the Church both to remit and to retain sins, and the exercise of that Commission by the Church through her ministry, are, to say the least, biologically scientific. That which was won for all must be assigned to each. The power of the Resurrection —like life itself—needs for effectiveness to be individuated. "By His authority committed unto me, I absolve" is, like Baptism and Communion, a corporate act of individuation. That in many cases it provides exactly what is requisite to meet a real need for life must be obvious to those who know anything about these things.

won complete freedom by complete control over that most proximate environment of all, His own body. At will He could materialize and dematerialize an appropriate instrument for functioning in this material world. This I take to be the goal of the age-long process towards freedom by increase of faculty and towards individuality by multiplication of relationships. "Go ye into all the world and preach the gospel *to every creature*" is the outlook of Him Who as Man won perfect individuality, and with it, "the power of an endless life."

This is the goal, but the goal is not the finish. After the great forty days came the Ascension, inexhaustibly suggestive. There must be other planes of existence in the Universe than that to which our earth life has introduced us. These too are open to man—not at once perhaps, but only after many days of further progress, progress until on every plane and in every part of the mighty whole he can express, as his very own, that particle of the Conscious Energy of the world, with which he was entrusted, with an appropriate instrument, of his own creating, for wheresoever he may wish to be.

The final revelation was given in terms of time and space, perhaps to warn us that these are more eternal than some are apt to think. Time and space are, it may be, only modes of thought but likely enough they are the only modes in which individual persons can ever think.

"In My Father's House are many mansions"—many and "mansions," not very little rooms. None of them, perhaps, less than a great planet. The world to come is the immensity of the Universe itself. But we shall not be lost in it, for we shall share in the largeness of Him Who bid us be of good cheer, because it was the Universe itself that He had conquered.

As in the case of Our Lord's Passion, it is to the magnificent hymns of the early centuries that we must go to find the sort of touch of passionate reality which belongs to a religion so Catholic that it finds God everywhere and sees the whole world as one continuous divine process. Here is one that comes down to us from the fifth century:—

"Eternal Monarch, King most high,
Whose Blood hath brought redemption nigh,
By Whom the death of Death was wrought,
And conquering grace's battle wrought.

Yea, Angels tremble when they see
How changed is our humanity;
That flesh hath purged what flesh had stained,
And God, the Flesh of God, hath reigned.

Be Thou our joy and strong defence,
Who art our future recompense,
So shall the light that springs from Thee
Be ours through all eternity.

VIII.

"It is God who delivered us out of the dominion of darkness, and has transferred us into the Kingdom of His dearly beloved Son, in whom we have our redemption—the forgiveness of our sins. Christ is the visible representation of the invisible God, the Firstborn and Lord of all creation. For in Him was created the universe of things, in heaven and on earth, things seen and things unseen, thrones, dominions, princedoms, powers—all were created, and exist, through and for Him. And He is before all things, and in and through Him the universe is one harmonius whole," not a static multiverse but a dynamic universe.

I add this line to Dr. Weymouth's translation of Colossians I., 13—17, as it shows how Pauline is the outlook of modern science or, if you like, how modern in his outlook is S. Paul. *God has delivered us out of the dominion of darkness*—that fatal *impasse* of the law of no retrogression; *into the Kingdom of His dearly beloved Son*—the line of man's true evolution towards, freedom, individuality, perfection; *in Whom we have our redemption, the forgiveness of our sins*—it really was a case of rescue, something cosmic must needs have happened, sin had to be unrivetted from doom. *Things seen and unseen, thrones, dominions, princedoms, powers*—here we have all that can be packed into Nature's *continuum*, the germ-plasm of modern science and all that I have ventured to speculate upon under the name "Organic Evolution's Mental Concomitant" and to think of as the gradually individuating Conscious Energy of the Universe. Surely something not less than *a power* expresses itself through the bees and something not less than *a dominion* through each great species of the animal world!

Next time you sing or hear the *Benedicite* and call upon all the works of the Lord to bless the Lord, don't think only of the green things or of the beasts and cattle alone, but include in your reverent thinkings the angels and powers and dominions of the individuating Consciousness of the Universe that they represent. You will find the hymn ten times more suggestive to you than it was before because you yourself have grasped a bit more of reality.

But of course "ancient and modern" in the way of outlook meet, as they meet no where else in the New Testament, in Romans VIII., 18 and following verses. S. Paul has just thought of us as children of God; "and if children, then heirs too—heirs of God and co-heirs with Christ." He writes as one amazed by the greatness of the prospect. Again I quote from Dr. Weymouth's translation. "Why, the sufferings of the present I deem not worth considering compared with the glory soon to be disclosed to us. All creation is yearning, longing, to see the manifestation of the sons of God. For the creation was made subject to futility, not of its own choice, but by the will of Him who so subjected it; yet with the hope that at last the creation itself would be set free from the thraldom of decay to enjoy the liberty that comes with the glory of the children of God. For we know that the whole creation is moaning in the pangs of child-birth until this hour. And more than that, we ourselves, though we possess the Spirit as a foretaste of bliss, yet we ourselves inwardly moan as we wait for full sonship in the redemption of our bodies."

Our bodies—our most proximate environment of all—the instrument which, with our physical brain, keeps us here and now within those limitations which are, presumably , essential for the making of a self by itself. Over His body, Perfect Man, "the Firstborn from the dead," evidenced by His Resurrection that He had won complete freedom by control. He won it by His own human might and right, as the achiever in His own Person of that divine sonship which is the end and aim of our whole organic process. We are still waiting for full sonship, which will mean for us also a like freedom to make for ourselves the appropriate instrument, wherein to function in that life of the world to came for which, were it not for His Cross and the gift of His Spirit of Sonship, we never could have qualified ourselves at all.

In an earlier section of my argument (page 45) I wrote "Everything below man in the scale of life has as a matter of fact at some time or other turned out of the main stream and left the narrow upward path by *error.*" I put it like that because I wanted to compare with what all organisms below man have done what man has done on the level of self-consciousness by sin. S. Paul puts it differently and much better. From the point of view of the organism, it was a futile proceeding to turn out of the main stream of life and settle down to equilibrium. But it really had no choice. It settled down by the will of Him who so subjected it. But for the turning aside of the vegetables from the main stream which led on to the animal world, there could have been no animal world; but for the turning aside of species after species of the animal world from the main stream which led on to man, there could have been no man. From the point of view of Him who wills the whole, it was not futile at all. And the fact that what was, from the point or view of the lower organisms, an error, was also from the point of view of its Author, essential to the whole process, fills S. Paul with a truly immense hope—the hope that at the last the Creation itself shall be set free from the thraldom of decay to enjoy "the liberty that comes with the glory of the children of God."

There are many who feel that the world to come will be defective in something of real value if none of those friendships which we may have formed with brothers and sisters, lower in the scale of evolution than we, can be picked up again hereafter. I imagine that S. Paul, in exegesis of his own great hope, would not have thought it irrational to suppose that, just as our own conscious friendship with God is guarantee of our own immortality, so the friends of those who reach "the liberty of the glory of the children of God" may be, by ourselves perhaps, recalled into being to enjoy with us that liberty. "It is," says S. Paul, "by hope that we have been saved"; who knows how many others, of like and of different degree, we may be able by our hope to include in our own salvation? Few of us are in danger of hoping too much!

The thraldom of decay—for some reason, when he came to I. Cor., xv., 42, Dr. Weymouth, instead of rendering the same Greek word "it is sown in decay," put instead, "the body is sown perishable." Our old Authorised Version, with more accuracy, keeps in both places the same English word for the same Greek word—"the bondage of corruption" and "it is sown in corruption." What is it, we may well ask, that is sown in corruption—corruption which S. Paul calls the bondage or thraldom of the world of Nature?

We are so accustomed to hear the passage read at a Burial Service that we slip into the way of thinking that S. Paul is referring to a dead human body. I doubt myself if such a thought ever passed through S. Paul's mind at all and perhaps no one would be more surprised than he to find that his analogy had ever been so interpreted. "But someone will say," he writes, "How do the dead rise. And with what kind of body do they come back? Foolish man! The seed you yourself sow does not come to life unless it dies: and what you sow is not the body which is to be, but a bare grain of wheat (it may be) or something else." But obviously *the whole point lies in there being in the grain of wheat exactly what there is not in a human corpse*—life. Not a grain of wheat, but the husk of a grain of wheat is like a dead body. No one expects to get anything from sowing husks! Something with life in it is sown, something which by death, passes to a larger life and gains a new body.

Recall the purpose of the material world into which, with the necessary limitations of an inherited body and a great bundle of faculties (representing, it may be, the condensed experience of millions of individuals) something is somehow plunged to create a self, and in connection with S. Paul's analogy, you will find much food for thought. The child is born— "The body is sown perishable, it rises imperishable: it is sown in dishonour, it rises in glory: it is sown in weakness, it rises in power: it is sown an animal body, it is raised a spiritual body."

A spiritual body—a body like that with which Our Lord rose from the dead. Not, that is a body made of spirit (which perhaps means nothing) but with a Spiritual Energy which can at will fashion its own appropriate instrument for self-expression. To make such a spirit body, or self, or character is the very purpose of our burial in a material world therein and thereby to win the freedom of the Universe—"the liberty of the glory," as S. Paul calls it, "of the children of God."

It is tempting to pursue my exposition of S. Paul from the evolutionary point of view; but my only wish is to suggest a line of thought which may be commoner than I fancy that it is. Once one's mind is in this direction, it is wonderful how the conviction grows that S. Paul was not only the first of modern psychologists but the first of modern biologists also, with a biology with much to say about life both in this world and in the world to come. At any rate it is a great thing to recognise that he is talking, in rather different language perhaps, about the same things that Science talks about to-day, and means by life life and by death death in their ordinary and accepted sense.

"To the man who has never known or experienced anything in his life for which he is willing to die, immortality must ever be a chimera."—J. Y. S.

Along the Curve.

I.

If through Christian telescopes we follow along our curve aright, I wrote in my introduction, we ought to come across items of evidence in the deposits of our Scriptures corroborative of any resulting theory and to find fresh light in explanation of some of those incidents recorded in connection with the life of Our Lord which puzzle many minds. Some of these incidents the last chapter has dealt with. In this I will merely select one or two out of a multitude of our Lord's teachings which suggest, at any rate, that if we extrapolate forwards the curve of what we know about evolution, it takes us in the right direction.

That the way of life is an upwards way involving effort; that all which tempts a man to settle down contentedly and find equilibrium in this world's comfort is a great danger; that a faith which will make ventures and centre itself upon God is all important, these points need no stressing. But the urgency with which Our Lord insists upon the *sine qua non* of love and kindliness, of consideration for others and above all of forgivingness, if we are even to begin to qualify for eternal life, arrests attention.

Evolution has tended throughout to greater and greater individuality through wider and wider relationships. Nature made the family in order to begin to make the individual. Some of Our Lord's sayings, which startle us at first, are really suggestions that the way to eternal life lies in the direction of widening out "the charities of home" till they embrace neighbours as well as relations. "Then said one unto him, behold thy mother and thy brethren stand without, desiring to speak with thee. But he answered and said unto him that told him, Who is my mother? and who are my brethren? And he stretched forth his hand toward his disciples, and said, Behold my mother and my brethren! For whosoever shall do the will of my Father which is in heaven, the same is my brother and sister and mother." (S. Matt. xii., 47-50). It was not that the perfect Son loved His Mother less, but that the circle of His family and the wealth and warmth of His affections included all the children of God.

I expect we far too easily persuade ourselves that Christian love is different in kind somehow from family love, just as we persuade ourselves that spiritual life means something altogether different from the life, the science of which we call biology, Love twixt a boy and a girl is the divinest thing in the world; but unless we are in the way towards widening out our affections here, we are not in the way towards that life wherein "they neither marry nor are given in marriage, but are as the angels of God in heaven."

This does not, of course, mean that the love of husband for wife and of wife for husband must cease to be. This was the love which, with the gift of children, evolution chose to be the spring of the whole movement towards individuation by the multiplying of relationships. To take this out of the world to come would make it fundamentally poorer than the world that is. But in the world to come, like all else that we carry on with us, the natural love of our family relationships must be the germ of something richer and fuller and wider to suit the measures of eternity. "We know that we have passed from death unto life, because we love the brethren" (I. S. John, iii., 14), is the one sufficient evidence that we have got back into the true line of evolution and are on the way to make a self with eternal value.

II.

To make a soul or self with eternal value—if this is the purpose of our world's process, we should expect to find something about it in Our Lord's teaching and indeed we do. "Jesus Christ," writes Professor Simpson "set before men the conditions of life or of death in the ultimate senses of these words, warning them of the difficulty of attaining life. 'Enter ye in by the narrow gate; for wide is the gate and broad is the way that leadeth to destruction, and many be they that enter in thereby. For narrow is the gate and straightened the way that leadeth unto life, and few be they that find it.' In clearest and sharpest contrast Jesus distinguishes between the alternatives, "life" and "destruction." Similarly in majestic simplicity and unassailable directness, He says: 'whosoever would save his soul or life shall lose it; and whosoever shall lose his life for my sake and the gospel's shall save it.' " "By the soul or life" adds Professor Simpson, "Jesus means the core of a man's personality, his very self, the citadel of his being. It is something charged with potentiality and a capacity for self-realization, something that may be won."

With the statement that it means "a man's very self," as with the statement that it is something that may be won or lost, I fully agree. It is all that is a man's very own, all that he himself creates, the whole bundle of his own thoughts, words and deeds. I am not sure that "the core of a man's personality" and "the citadel of his being" are not something larger and that it is not better to say that it is in the citadel of his being that a man must make his self. Clearly it is his self that matters to a man. If in the end he is mulcted of this, to gain the whole world would be as futile as it must be impossible.

"In your patience ye shall win your souls" said our Lord (S. Luke xxi., 19). It is typical of the translators of our Authorised Version that instead of "win" or "gain," which the Greek word certainly means, they put "possess." They were dominated

---

* "Man and the Attainment of Immortality," page 285.

by the theory of the inherent immortality of souls. Historically this is understandable, though it is really difficult to find in the New Testament itself anything that even looks like unconditional immortality. The theory found support from Plato, who arrived at it himself by arguments which do not seem to us very convincing. The argument amounts to this:—Ideas, or at any rate some ideas (*e.g.*, ideas of the good, the true and the beautiful) are eternal; if men's souls have these ideas in them, then the souls are immortal. (The Dialogues of Plato, Vol. I., p. 377, Jowett).

I am not sure that Christianity did not make room for the theory of unconditional immortality because without it it was impossible to believe in eternal punishment. As Dr. A. H. McNeile says, "The argument from Scripture cannot be that because the soul is essentially immortal punishment must be endless, but the converse—because Scripture teaches that punishment is endless, the soul must be immortal in order to suffer it."* Euclid might almost have added *quod est absurdum*. From end to end of the New Testament—from "the chaff He will burn up" to "He that hath the Son hath life and he that hath not the Son hath not life," immortality is conditional.

Had the New Testament taught the doctrine of inherent immortality, it would indeed have been a

* "The Problem of the Future Life," page 121.

difficult book for the evolutionist, who cannot help noting that, as far as God has revealed Himself as the Life of the world's organic process, His urge to every organism is to qualify itself, and largely by its own efforts, for each further advance. S. Paul notes the continuance of the same method with regard to man:—"Work out your own salvation with fear and trembling, for it is God that worketh in you both to will and to work, for his good pleasure." God's good pleasure is the evolution of sons.

III.

That there are verses in the New Testament, that there are among the recorded sayings of Our Lord Himself sentences which can be quoted as evidence for eternal punishment, I have no wish to deny. But they are extraordinarily few—extraordinarly few, considering that Jewish Apocalyptic, itself the child of times of persecution, was full of the idea and of imagery thereanent. Dr. A. H. McNeile does not in the least overstate the case when he says * that "The literal temporal force of 'everlasting' in Our Lord's words must be balanced by the deeper qualitative meaning which He gave to it. If this is done, and if, as is possible or probable, His apocalyptic language has been heightened in Christian tradition, there is not much beyond the stern Jewish symbolism in *Jude* and the *Revelation* to form the scriptural basis of the doctrine of endless punishment."

---

* Op cit, page 122.

There is no denying, I think, that judged pragmatically the doctrine of eternal punishment has not made for righteousness. Indeed it is difficult to believe that the Church of Jesus Christ could ever have adopted the role of persecutor or have justified to itself, even in its darkest ages, the torture of anyone, however heretical or bad, had it not thought that dreadful retribution hereafter was after the mind of God—retribution so dreadful that man's brief torturings were by comparison inconsiderable, indeed humane if they saved the temporal sufferer from an eternity in the fires of God.

Of useless retributory punishment God's great book of Nature knows absolutely nothing; about the non-survival of those who are not fit to survive she knows a great deal. It is an inevitable law of her whole process. It is only because a law of the organic process has been cancelled on his behalf that man, having proved himself unfit, yet has the opportunity to try again. It is an opportunity, but he must walk wisely and buy it up, as S. Paul says, if he would have it.

The stress of Our Lord's teaching—direct, solemn, even severe—is on the danger, not of eternal punishment, but of destruction—*destruction of the self*. "Those who believe in conditional immortality," says Dr. McNeile, "think that when Our Lord spoke of destruction by fire, He intended to teach annihilation, stress being laid on the simile of the burning of vegetables, which cannot feel pain: trees (Matt. iii., 10—Luke iii., 9), chaff (Matt. iii., 12 —Luke iii., 17), tares (Matt. xiii., 40), branches (John xv., 6)." I cannot see how anyone can imagine that these similes were intended to teach anything else.

That in the Universe there is and must be something of which "eternal fire" is no exaggerating figure, is, I think, clear enough. By some process the rubbish is in the end always and everywhere burnt up. Much rubbish is part of the mixed character that most of us make while in this world and into the eternal fire the rubbish will go, even when the self has made itself with survival value.

If, however, the self has, by the grace of God, made itself with survival value, there is no reason whatever to suppose that it will stay in the eternal fire. Quite the contrary; purged and purified it will come out of it. The whole conception is, of course, a great figure; but it is a true figure, about which God's great Book of Nature and God's great Book of the written word say the same.

Was S. Paul thinking, I wonder, along these lines when he wrote (I. Cor. iii., 11—15) "Other foundation can no man lay than that which is laid, which is Jesus Christ. But if any man buildeth on the foundation gold, silver, costly stones, wood, hay, stubble; each man's work shall be made manifest; for the day shall declare it, because it is revealed in fire; and the fire shall prove each man's work of what sort it is. If any man's work shall abide which he built thereon, he shall receive a reward. If any man's work shall be burned, he shall suffer loss: but he *himself* shall be saved; yet so as through fire." The great danger is lest a man make a self which itself cannot survive, not because God does not wish it to survive, but because in the very nature of things it has no survival value.

Here again Nature and the Bible are at one in the suggestion that an inevitable destruction of a soul or self may be, perhaps must be, a painful process. When organisms quite low down in the scale of life cease to survive, because they are not fit to survive, pain, or something like pain, marks the process. Neither in the Bible nor in Nature is there anything that ought to lead us unconcernedly to suppose that nothing worse than painless extinction awaits those who in this world have sold their birthright for a mess of pottage.

IV.

No one, who accepts Our Lord's teaching, or who sees in evolution the expression work of "the Word" who "was made flesh" can do otherwise than regard our life here and now as momentous. Unless something is going on here and now of immense importance, something which, if it goes wrong here, cannot be put right elsewhere, then so stupendous a happening as the Incarnation really is incredible.

Unless in the course of man's normal three score years and ten, or some lesser period it may be, he is making something which cannot be made under other conditions and cannot be made in simpler and easier ways, we are not dealing with reality at all. It is partly the easy-going assumption that in spiritual matters things can easily be rectified (either here or elsewhere, if not here) that makes so much of our religion seem so unreal.

A self is the outcome of its own reactions to its own environment; it is literally created by its own experience; there can be no "pretend" about it, no "make believe" that things which do matter don't matter. Reality knows nothing whatever of pretence, and spiritual things are not less real than are things material.

God Himself cannot do what He has made to be impossible, nor do we honour Him by supposing that He can. He cannot make that which, by its very meaning, only itself can make itself. As I ventured to say in my *A Soul in the Making*, when God did make the Perfect Human Person, *He did not make, He became*. God can and does provide the materials, the opportunity, the urge, the energy and, by His own Self-limitation, room and scope for freedom; but there is no getting away from the trite but true saying that as surely as acts make habits and habits character, so does character—our own character—make our destiny. True repentance is not something apart from character—it means a fundamental change of mind.

If through its own fault a self makes itself without survival value, or even if through no fault there is no survival value, that self cannot survive. The most that can be looked for by a Christian Biologist (and it may be looked for surely with good hope) is what Mr. McDowall, in the last Chapter of his *Evolution and the Need of Atonement* speaks of as "*other larval existences.*"

V.

In the most interesting chapter (Chapter IX.) on *The Evolution of Individuality* in his *Man and the Attainment of Immortality*, Professor Simpson raises the question whether the human social organism or the State constitutes the chief end of the whole organic process; whether the State should be regarded as the true Individual, in relation to which the individuals, who compose the State, find their *raison d'être* and by incorporation with which they achieve their end. He concludes that "no comparison is possible between the perfect social functioning of the cells of the normal organism and the activities of the individuals composing a State. The interests of the individuals are not alike: they are even antagonistic, as when the latter are considered as grouped in different so-called "classes." When I first read this chapter some three years ago I made a note in pencil at the end of it—'*if not the State? the Church.*'

Certainly in its history so far the Church has shown itself to be a dividual rather than an individual. None the less, with a magnificent anticipation of faith, the Church goes on saying day by day "I believe that there is One Holy Catholic Church, a Communion of Saints," *one* in the mind and purpose of God in spite of all that man has done to mar its unity, *holy* in spite of all that has soiled its holiness, *catholic* in spite of the narrow limits of its outlook and effective energy.

That the curve of organic evolution should seem to go on in the direction of some perfect social organization, though no perfect social organization has yet appeared in the realm of facts with which Science deals, is for faith much more than interesting. It is the business of faith to make present in thought what is still future in fact, and it hardly needs to be pointed out that to S. Paul's mind over and over again the climax is just what Professor Simpson adumbrates as the possible end of the evolutionary process—a perfect society, thought of as the body, of which Christ is the head, "from whom all the body fitly framed and knit together through that which every joint supplieth, according to the working in due measure of each several part, maketh the increase of the body unto the building up of itself in love" (Eph. iv., 16). Only "all together," as S. Paul sees it, can we each attain *ἐις ἄνδρα τέλειον*, unto a perfectly evolved man, unto the measure of the stature of the fulness of Christ. Christian faith anticipated by two thousand years the latest and best surmisings of Evolution as to the end of its process—an end to be reached, it may be, only after many ages yet and only in a world to come.

In speaking just now of the life of the world to come I said that the love of husband and wife was the love which, with the gift of children, evolution chose to be the spring of her whole movement towards individuation by multiplication of relationships. I added that in the world to come, like all else that we carry on with us, the natural love of our family relationships must be the germ of something richer and wider to fit the measures of eternity. When hereafter the sort of love, which began first of all perhaps in the union of two cells and has been the chief spring of progress ever since, reaches in intensity and extensity its end and perfection, there will be at last, not in faith, but in fact, "a glorious Church, not having spot or wrinkle or any such thing."

Again, for faith it is something more than interesting, to note that S. Paul's most glowing picture of the Church as she is to be, forms the centre of his homely teachings about how those who are married ought to feel and behave towards each other. "Husbands ought also to love their own wives as their own bodies . . . even as Christ also the Church; because we are members of His body." "This mystery," he adds, "is great; but I speak in regard of Christ and of the Church." (Eph. v., 32). It is great indeed; for here we are at the heart of the world.*

Far, far back at the very beginning of organic life affinities between elementary organisms began—humble enough at first. Thus the Conscious Energy of the World initiated the process, which step by step led on to our Christian family—twain becoming one flesh—which will find its consummation hereafter in the Body (perfectly knit together by love)

* About the potencies of married love S. Paul has some very interesting speculations in I. Cor. vii., "How knowest thou, O wife, whether thou shalt save thy husband? or how knowest thou, O husband whether thou shalt save thy wife? (v., 16). It is superficial, I think, to interprpet this as merely meaning that the husband or wife married to a Christian is in the best environment for conversion, especially after verse 14, where he says that "the unbelieving husband is sanctified in the wife and the unbelieving wife is sanctified in the brother." The oldest, best, deepest, most potent of all loves is the love of husband and wife, and what S. Paul says at least suggests to me that such love needs for its completion hereafter continuance of lover and loved and that, if one of the twain achieves eternal value, he or she may somehow do for the other what she or he may have failed to do for themselves. The love of husband and wife, with the gift of children is, as I have said, the dynamic which evolution chose for all higher progress and out of it have grown all the charities of home and neighbourhood and Church. I see no reason to exclude from my thinkings the hope that the love of anyone, who makes a self with eternal value, may prove to have saving power for others. Naturally I am most conversant with the work of parish priests. It is quite manifest that the parish priest who saves, is the parish priest who really loves his people one by one. Love—the ordinary love of our everyday affections—is always and everywhere a saving grace.

of Him from Whom all things took their origin and in Whom all will find their end. What exactly S. Paul had in his mind throughout this passage it is impossible to say; but unless he did somehow glimpse something of what we see that the love of man and wife is, both in evolutionary retrospect and prospect, it is difficult to understand why the mystery of Christ and the Church is used in this connection at all.

If, as would seem to be the case, the love of parents for each other and for their children was the dynamic chosen by Evolution for progress towards that "individuation by multiplication of relationships" which is the necessary qualification for the survival of a soul, it is easy to understand why Christianity sets its face so sternly against divorce. Back of all the fundamental doctrines of the Catholic Religion is always something in the very constitution of the Universe. This is why some sins of the flesh bring immediate and curiously poignant remorse; they are up against the main stream of life. Man's true line of Evolution is broken by breach of wedlock. Of the self of those who break it, Evolution without pity seals the doom. For them, of course, as for others, the Cross has hewn a way back; but none walk in that way save by true repentance.

The Church of Rome is scientifically right in refusing to recognise divorce; but she is wise sometimes in her decision that this or that particular marriage was no true marriage. In spiritual matters rigid administration needs to be softened sometimes by the equity of dispensation and I should hold myself that what, by her spiritual authority, the Church looses on earth, is also loosed in heaven, by which I should understand in this connection, the very constitution of things. There are marriages which are no marriages, but are from the start tragedies in very slight disguise.

As a matter of fact human society, organised on Christian principles, has itself gone a very long way in the direction of defeating a fundamental law of evolution in its earlier stages—the law of the survival only of the fit. Christian Society spends much of its skill and energy on enabling the physically and mentally unfit to survive and sets an absolute value on individual life. It is perfectly right, for the true direction of evolution has been from the beginning towards increase of the "other-regarding instinct" and the decrease of the "self-regarding" instinct. But Society, having cancelled in very large measure the law of the survival of the fit, may find itself obliged, and certainly ought not to find itself blamed, if it takes steps to prevent the marriage of those who are mentally or physically unfit for the procreation of children. Social other-regarding instinct will have to be balanced by Social self-regarding instinct—at least biology seems to point in that direction. We have no power to alter the laws of life.

VI.

This mystery is great. What exactly is meant by a mystery in Christian terminology? One well-known definition of it is "a revealed secret." I think myself that this misses the point. The point of a mystery is that you cannot get at it by intellect or logic. It is something that, to be understood, must be *lived* into. It is not something that cannot be understood, but something that can only be understood by experience. Life is a mystery. The first condition for any understanding of life is that you must be alive yourself. Love is a mystery; when you have been in love yourself, you begin to know what it means. The education given by our older Universities is a mystery; you can only get into it by living at Oxford or Cambridge for three years. It has been well described as education by initiation in contrast with the education by illumination given by another and more modern type of University. The same is true of our old foundation Public Schools as compared with some of more modern type. The difficulty is to combine initiation with illumination! This really is the problem, our failure to solve which still necessitates our dual system of public education. It is a fundamental problem, and like other fundamental problems can never be got over except by being solved. It is very difficult, because those who have never themselves got into this mystery of education can hardly understand those who have.

Quite properly Christianity calls the great foundation facts of her faith mysteries—the Incarnation, the Cross, the Resurrection, the Ascension and Pentecost. To begin to understand them you must live your way into them in the experience of life. This is one of the paradoxes of Christianity—you must accept most of it in order to prove that any of it is true. In experience it becomes its own proof.

To the liberating outlook of evolution, nothing could seem to be less scientific or more perverse than the tacit assumption of many modernists and anti-modernists alike that, if some sort of antecedent to this or that doctrine or practice of developed Christianity can ingeniously be discovered in some previous religion, the discovery discredits this or that particular Christian doctrine or practice. To assume that Christianity is unique, in the sense that it is a thing altogether apart from men's pre-Christian thinkings, is to adopt towards it exactly the attitude adopted by a generation or more ago towards the suggestion, so familiar to us and so obviously true, that man is organic to nature. Our fathers and grandfathers thought that unless it could be shown that man was an entirely fresh creation and unique, somehow his whole dignity would be gone. It seems to us that the dignity of man is mightily enhanced by the fact that he represents the travail of a world and is himself the crown of an age-long process, the wonder of which and the immensity of which increase with our knowledge day by day.

We do not really honour Christianity by looking upon it as a unique extra, hardly to be thought of in connection with man's evolution. "The Cross," wrote Mrs. E. Herman, in her *The Meaning and Value of Mysticism*, "is the ground plan of the Great Architect of the Universe," and an older work spoke of "the Lamb slain from the foundation of the world." The Eternal Word did not begin to function on Christmas Day.

Christianity is the explanation of the world and of the world's organic process. It gathers up into itself and sublimates all that men have tried to express in all manner of ways as they felt after God if haply they might find Him. The Mystery Religions —the best religions of the old world—were full of ideas and disciplines which have found their fulfilment in Christianity. What evidence we have goes to show that they were often crudely, even brutally expressed, but, then, I have often thought that a service in old Israel at which ten thousand beasts were slaughtered, must have been a very horrid service! Surely no Christian should be surprised to find, *e.g.*, in the myths of Isis and Osiris, ideas about life and death and resurrection akin to those of our religion. The surprising thing would be if we did not find them there and elsewhere.* Catholic means as large as the Universe, and any religion which claims that great title must gather into itself all the longings and gropings of men since men began to think.

* See also Bishop Gore's "The Holy Spirit in the Church," Chapter iii. Section i.

I remember once getting a letter from a rather violent protestant to the effect that the Cross was nothing but a pagan symbol. If the writer had struck out the words "nothing but" I could easily have agreed with him. Plato uses the Cross as a symbol and so did the Egyptians. Had they never glimpsed anything of the ground plan of the world in which they lived, it would have been strange indeed.

I believe myself that the venerable rule of fasting before Communion either came into the Church from the Mystery Religions or was, at any rate, the lineal descendant of a similar act of self-discipline, enjoined upon those who wished to qualify for their more important ceremonies. The fact that fasting, as well as prayer, is in our Prayer Book enjoined for an adult candidate for Baptism, can set us thinking in the right direction. The fact, too, that it, or something like it, has probably obtained ever since man began to think seriously about religion, accounts for the emotion which is often discharged if the validity of the rule is even tentatively called in question. A religious complex of immense antiquity is exploded. I use the word complex psychologically and not derogatively. Some complexes are most valuable. It also accounts for the disproportionate value which seems to be set sometimes on what is sometimes rationalised on manifestly insufficient grounds.

The true ground is a scientific and really important one. To be in the best condition for passing through the material to the spiritual, you must not be digesting food. He is in the best condition to make the best Communion who is fasting, if his bodily health allows it, just as the candidate for Baptism had better be fasting. It is a qualitative and enabling rule.

That the practice is of immense antiquity, that it has been enjoined as the right preliminary to other ceremonies besides the Eucharist, that it rests ultimately on a scientific basis—on a psycho-physical basis if you like—does not make me value it less but more.* But it does make it, I think, unjustifiable to exalt an admirable disciplinary rule into a moral commandment or to suggest that the partaking of any sort of nourishment within so many hours disqualifies for a good Communion. In some cases the breach of the rule is more reverent than the observance.

I have always wished that a body of competent scholars would go into the whole question. I believe

* For the same sort of reasons I set immense store by incense. Smell is the least intellectualised of our five senses and the directest route to our subconscious. Without our being aware of it, the smell of a place is a prime factor in the impression that it makes on us. The impression left upon us by some cathedrals of coldness and dead-aliveness is, I am convinced, largely made upon us by their smell—the smell of mere antiquity. Every Sunday morning, when I am at home, I go round our cathedral early and cense every altar. It makes a world of difference to the feel of the whole place. It is difficult not to say your prayers in a place about which hangs the scent of incense. Call it magical, if you like, but it is the magic of divine science. For more about this I may perhaps refer my reader to my "The Nature of a Cathedral," page 57.

that it would find that what is adumbrated here is true and that it points in the right direction for the solving of what is a very real problem to very many people under the conditions of modern life. I believe I am right in saying that the Church of Rome has already moved cautiously in the direction of relaxing the rule in certain specified cases. I number among my friends more than one priest of our Church of England, who by mid day on a Sunday is physically worn out, after perhaps three or even four Celebrations in a large parish, to the detriment alike of his health and of his temper. For such, it seems to me, the Church which with motherly wisdom binds, should with discreet insistence loose. Other ordinances, besides the Sabbath, were made for man—because they are meant to be good for him. Rigidity is good for no one.

I have quoted one sentence from Mrs. Herman's rather difficult but extraordinarily suggestive book, *The Meaning and Value of Mysticism.* I close this section with a paragraph (page 338). "The Cross is not an after-thought of God—a heroic remedy for a desperate emergency—but the corner stone of creation. If the Christ process must be repeated in every human soul; if no Son of God can be brought to glory except he be crucified with Christ as well as believe in Christ crucified for him; nay if the whole cosmos must travel to God by way of Calvary, then the Cross is the heart of the Universe—is, indeed, none other than that meek omnipotence of God by which chaos is being turned to order and evil to good. . . . . If we realise that God is love and that His omnipotence, wisdom and justice are the omnipotence, wisdom and justice of perfect love, we must sooner or later arrive at the doctrine of the essential humanity, or rather Christhood, of God, and see in the death of Jesus, not the veiling, but the most perfect manifestation of His glory." "He realised in every particular that towards which the whole evolutionary process has been evidently tending." So Professor Simpson sums it up. In Him eternally, to quote a famous line from Sir Edwin Arnold's *The Light of Asia*, "foregoing self the Universe grows I."

VII.

Integral with Christianity are the two great Sacraments of the Gospel. The Church calls them mysteries. They are mysteries in the proper sense of that word. Try to intellectualise them, and you become hopelessly superficial; live them, and you find yourself an initiate on the way to understanding.

Both Holy Baptism and the Eucharist are dramatic symbols and instruments of corporate individuation—of individuation (to use once more an often repeated phrase) by multiplication of relationships. By the one, individually "incorporated into the Holy Church," in the other, the Christian initiate prays that "with Thy whole Church" we may receive remission of our sins and all other benefits of our Lord's Passion. Both express dramatically and in symbol—as only it can be expressed—the Heart of the Universe. It was a great saying of Goethe's that "the highest cannot be spoken." It can only be acted.

"The bread of God is that which cometh down out of heaven and giveth life unto the world" (S. John, vi., 33). We spoil it all if we let ourselves think that there are different sorts of life and that life here means something different from the life about which biology has taught us a very great deal. All life is the gift of the Bread of God. Life expresses itself on different levels; but the life in an amoeba is the same life which expresses itself more fully in man. This is the meaning of the whole process and this is the meaning of the Christian Eucharist. It is the meaning of the Cross itself. On Good Friday there flashed into the world *in human terms* the eternal meaning of the Universe.

"The breaking of bread"—bread, the staff of life and wine "which maketh glad the heart of man." Could there be more suggestive symbols of more abundant life by death? Golden grains of wheat are literally golden sunshine; but to become the staff of life, they must be ground to powder, baked by fire, killed, eaten, digested. As with the wheat, so with the wine. On the hillsides the grapes store up the sunshine, and they must be crushed, fermented, killed, assimilated—so only can they be transformed into the energy of a more abundant life. Unless for us there is a Real Presence of Christ in the bread and in the wine before as well as after its consecration, we miss the heart of the mystery.* We miss it, too, unless we recognise throughout that *it is the Eucharist*, holding together in our immediate thinkings Good Friday and Easter Day. The whole great organic process, from end to end, is alive from the dead through Jesus Christ our Lord. Good Friday is always next to Easter Even.

Christianity is the explanation of the world—no wonder that its central act of worship is a great drama—the drama of the Universe and of Him Whose death is the life of the Universe which He has conquered for Himself. If on one side is death, on the other side is life, no more distant from each other or divisible from each other than are the convex and concave of the curve, the forwards extrapolation of which is the movement of this book.

VIII.

In the Baptistery of our Cathedral Church of Chester stands a great font. It was brought to us from Italy. It is some 1,200 years old. It is large enough for a Baptism by immersion. It is indeed *a tomb hewn out of a rock*, designed for the Christian initiate's burial with Christ beneath the water and for his rising with Him to newness of life—a dramatic and symbolic presentation at the outset of all that is

---

* In another connection Mr. Studdert Kennedy has put this admirably in Chapter vi. of his "The Word and the Work."

to be experienced in life. I say a dramatic and symbolic presentation—this it certainly is and, I believe myself, much more, best described as the establishment, on the level of faith and reality, of that identification of the baptized with Christ Himself, which is the meaning of the Christian life and due to be the outcome of incorporation into Christ's Body. What our brethren of the sixth century felt about it, they made plain by their decoration of our font. They covered it all over with wonderful patterns and peacocks. To be swept into the Christ life of His Body, the Church, seemed to them such a gorgeous thing that nothing less gorgeous than a peacock's tail could adequately represent it. It is exactly this *feel* that we of to-day need to recover, wherewith to freshen up the dutiful prosiness of very much of our religion.

In connection with the healing of bodily and moral ills, M. Coué, interpreted by M. Baudouin and others, has familiarised us all with the terms "hetero" and "auto" suggestion—*i.e.*, suggestion made to someone by someone else, and suggestion made to someone by someone's self. He has also taught us that, to be effective, every hetero-suggestion must be turned into an auto-suggestion by the individual patient. But suggestion is potent in every sphere of conscious life, and in none more than in the sphere of religion, which has to do with much more of our complex selves than our intellectual faculty. Sacraments are inevitably great hetero-suggestions, *divine*, I believe, as well as human, and they do not lose any of their divineness if, through psychology, we begin to understand, at least in part, how they work.

From the point of view of evolution, as I conceive it, there is something to be said by Science as well as by Tradition in favour of infant baptism. It was Weismann who insisted, probably over insisted, that the creative machinery of evolution lies in the womb of the germ-plasm to be worked out undisturbed by the surrounding conditions of life. At least it seems to be certain that any permanent modification of an organism must begin as modification of the germ-plasm. I myself believe, as I have argued at some length, that facts require us to let into our thinkings the idea at least of some individuating mental concomitant of the germ-plasm itself. Perhaps most of us, without recognising it, are assuming the existence of something of the kind when we allow ourselves to talk about the Sub-conscious. I can see no reason why if there can be dynamic modifications in the germ-plasm, there may not be also dynamic impressions on its invisible mental concomitant, impressions all more likely to be deep and permanent if made early and unmodified by the conscious self.*

If a baptism is a real happening, I find myself obliged to think that it must make a great difference whether or no the baptised infant is surrounded by corporate faith, and prayer and thought. But if the

* See Note at the end of this Chapter.

baptism is in fact the corporate hetero-suggestion of the divine society, which I believe the Church to be, if in the sacrament we are thinking God's thoughts after Him, then I see nothing unreasonable or unscientific in supposing that the baptised child sets out upon life with something in the depths of his being which "by nature he cannot have." For such a mass hetero-suggestion to the child's sub-conscious normally to be effective, it must later on be turned into an auto-suggestion by the child himself.*

It is its insistence on the necessity for faith on the part of their recipients that differentiates the sacraments of the Christian Church from many of the rites of the older Mystery Religions. To some of these the word *magical* in its debased sense might be applied. It is good, however, to recognise that in origin *magical* is not an evil word. It just means the wisdom of the East and Christianity itself came from the East. If by the word is meant the crude notion that certain acts or certain formulæ, correctly performed or repeated, command or compel unseen spiritual persons or forces, of course we are all against it. If, however, the word is used to describe everything in religion or out of it that does business with something deeper in man than his intellect, then the world is full of magic and would be a very poor

---

* The grand opportunity for putting the child, who was baptised as an infant into *the mental attiude* of an adult towards his baptism is of course his Confirmation. Thenceforwards in his habitual thinkings, his baptism, completed by his confirmation, should be the spring of his life. This is, I fancy, very often missed.

place without it. The most magical thing in the world is love. It is the one true Aladdin's Lamp! Again, if any suggestion that the Christian Sacraments are more than acted sermons, that something happens objectively, that their subjective impression upon the recipient is not the total of their reality, is to be called magic, then they are full of magic and always have been. Without defining what they mean by it, a good many people, it seems to me, talk a good deal of nonsense about magic, and having done so, proceed to label most of the things I value in life as magical! My own Cathedral of Chester is full of magic; that is why it is a joy for ever.

There is nothing of magic in the bad sense about the suggestion that such a corporate act of individuation as a Baptism, properly and prayerfully administered, makes an indelible mark for good on the sub-conscious of the recipient. Indeed scientific is a much more appropriate epithet to apply to it than magical. Nothing could be more scientific than to make a person at the outset what, by his co-operating faith, he must afterwards become. Everything in the world that lives is "made in order to become," from the chestnut that grows into the chestnut tree or the tadpole that becomes a frog, to the last baby whom I christened. Only of course in the case of a little self-conscious person-in-the-making, the person must be taught to grip, by his own dynamic anticipatory thought. what he was made in faith in order that he might become it in fact.

Dynamic anticipatory thought—this is the best working definition of faith that I know. It could not, I think, be put better than in our old Church Catechism—"My baptism, wherein I was made a member of Christ, the child of God and an inheritor of the kingdom of heaven." In faith I was made all three in order that I may become them in fact. If I get all three habitually present on the level of thought, all three will come true on the level of fact as if by magic, if you like; only it will be by the magic of God—by a law of your very being.

I have described Baptism as a dramatic and symbolic presentation at the outset of all that is to be experienced in the Christian life—the life which has got back into the main line of man's evolution. I doubt if we sufficiently appreciate the value of symbols. They are, I believe, the only possible centre of unity for a free association. The British Empire is held together by the symbol of the Crown. If we tried to replace it by a constitution on paper, the Empire would begin to go to pieces in a week. A formula is rigid; a symbol is free and you see in it just as much as you are capable of seeing, finding no ground of quarrel with your neighbours because one sees more and another less than you do. When in our English religion, formularies began to take the place of symbols, the splits began of which at last we are all ashamed. We do well to be ashamed of them. If Christianity is the true line of man's further evolution, the divisions of Christendom must be like great rocks that dam the stream of life. Till they are removed, the purpose of the Universe itself is held up—that "all together we may come unto the unity of the faith and of the knowledge of the Son of God unto a perfectly evolved man." We can hardly hope to recover unity in fact till we recover the true and scientific basis of unity in faith. The scientific and therefore divinely ordained basis of Christian unity is baptism, whereby we are made in faith all that we need ever hope or wish to become in fact.

"I believe that there is a Communion of Saints," in other words, I believe that all those who have ever been baptised, be they in the flesh or out of it, are one great family, brotherhood, communion for always and always—here is the old scientific basis. Neither some one visible Head, nor this or that form of government, however admirable or however venerable, can become a unifying centre for a free association. But to acknowledge one Baptism—a Baptism which makes my Roman Catholic and Eastern Orthodox brother, and my Presbyterian or Wesleyan brother equally with me and myself equally with them members of the Household of God, sheep of the one flock of the one Good Shepherd—thus to acknowledge one Baptism, is to have personally appropriated the one sure ground for hope for the Re-union of Christendom, if not in our own day, in that of our children's children. I doubt if we need anything more to-day than to restore Baptism to its Scriptural and rightful place in our habitual Christian thinkings—the scientific basis of Christian Unity.

It was the Life of the whole evolutionary process Who, just before the close of His earthly life, prayed "Sanctify them through thy truth . . . . . that they may be perfect in one." Till they are, the consummation cannot be reached. By Baptism we are, in faith, anticipatorily made one man in Jesus Christ. Fact waits for the world to come, but here in faith it must begin.

NOTE.

* Some children seem to be born with a special religious faculty and stand out quite distinctly in an often not particularly religious environment. For them religion is from the start a dominant interest. I have known many such. I get the impression (call it superstition, if you like) that they have come into the world with the impress of a baptism still fresh upon their sub-conscious. It may be thus that "children which are baptised, dying before they commit sin" (or have time to make any kind of self) "are undoubtedly saved." Experimental psychology seems to make it clear that a very young child is not a conscious self. With the exception of a few protective instincts, man's mental and spiritual life is of the nature of an acquirement. During the long and helpless period of infancy, the power of acquiring is itself but slowly maturing. This fact presents a very great difficulty except along the lines of thinking suggested in this book. I do not pretend that its lines of thinking have not difficulties of their own: but they are difficulties which can be thought out, with no ultimate loss to father or mother or child, but with perhaps much gain to all three. The conservation of a self, which has never existed, seems to me unthinkable. Somewhere a Self must make itself, and I believe that our earth is the Universe's Primary Factory of Souls.

Expecto.

I.

In my preface I said that my chief object in writing this book is to bring my readers, through a large portico, to the door of that portico which leads to the building beyond and to get them to look through it for themselves. That door we now approach deliberately. Of the building into which we are going to look, a Gothic Cathedral is no bad figure. Stand in it where you will and you can never see to the end of it; but delightful vistas—beyond and beyond and beyond—entice you in every direction. But please note that what you can actually see through the door is part of *a work of restoration*. It is important, I think, to remember this.

"We believe," writes Bishop Westcott in his *The Historic Faith* "that the Incarnation would have been necessary for the fulfilment of man's destiny even if he had perfectly followed the divine law"—if he had kept in his true line of evolution. "The Passion was necessary for the redemption of man fallen . . . . . . The idea of Christ's sufferings, the idea of redemption, pre-supposes the idea of a Fall. Such an idea is, I venture to say, a necessary condition of human hope. No view of life can be so inexpressibly sad as that which denies the Fall. If evil belongs to a man as man there appears to be no prospect of relief here or hereafter." To use a homely figure, if the blackness of sin was like the blackness of tar, an integral part of the material, it would be a desperate case. Happily it is like the blackness of soot in water, and so there is hope. To deny or to explain away the Fall is as biologically superficial as it is fundamentally non-Christian.

Our Lord has shown us, I believe, in His Transfiguration, the point at which, but for sin, humanity would have arrived on this earth. If we were able to pass on by transfiguration, instead of by death, the part of the building which we can see through our door would bear a different aspect. As it is, the fact that we must enter it by abnormal death and not by normal transfiguration, must mean that further development is needed before man reaches the stage at which, (but for having turned out of the true line of his evolution), he would have passed on from this earth. His environment in the immediate beyond must be a factor, perhaps the chief factor, in his restoration to normality.

Writing of man's evolution on earth, Professor Simpson says, "The developing organism and its environment react the one upon the other independently; yet in virtue of its adaptiveness the organism is progressively able to set itself free from the control of the physical environment and prove itself the more victorious of the two. Their separation, however, is practically impossible: *we are almost compelled to consider the organism and its environment as a single* *system undergoing change.** This must, I think, hold good of at least the restorative stages of our development in any life of any world to come.

It needs also to be remembered that personal identity is bound up with continuity. Clearly the achievement of personal identity is no easy matter. To make its achievement possible the material world was brought into existence. A life's experience works great changes. Between the child of six and the philosopher of sixty there is a world of difference; but personal identity is preserved because the change is both gradual and continuous. If the child of six was suddenly transformed into the philosopher at seven, they would not be the same people. The experience we call death must mean a great change, but, if our personal identity is to be preserved, we cannot ourselves be suddenly transformed into something or someone else. Into something or someone else we shall inevitably be transformed if our environment is suddenly and totally different from all that we have hitherto experienced. From birth to death organism and environment are best thought of as a single system undergoing change; after death the self and its environment must be a single system still. If I were suddenly to become an angelic being in a timeless and spaceless world, it would be no longer I.

I do not myself think that we begin to understand things till we realize that we live in a Universe or

---

* "Spiritual Interpretation of Nature," page 101.

single system and see that what are often called analogies are really identities on its different planes of life. Every year nature goes through its experience of death and resurrection. This is not an analogy of our Lord's Resurrection or of our own; it is identical with it on another plane of life, and Life always and everywhere is He. Year after year November and December come round, so dark and to some of us so dull. To nature they must be her time of times, for it is then that in her womb the wonderful things happen, of which the Spring is the annual evidence and delicious outcome. Every time that Nature is born again we marvel and rightly; what we have no business to marvel at is the fact that, being ourselves organic with Nature, we too need to be born again.

II.

"Marvel not that I said unto thee Ye must be born again" (S. John, iii., 5 and 7). If primarily we connect these words with our Baptism, most of us, I imagine, feel that their total significance and the total significance of the whole passage in which they occur, is by no means exhausted by that reference. I have no wish to belittle the greatness of Baptism, as my readers will have gathered from my section on that Sacrament. I believe that a Baptism is a real happening, that it does secure to the Christian child 'that which by nature he cannot have,' that the old word regeneration is not too strong a word to use of what is thereby done in faith that it may become actual in fact; but I expect to find that the re-birth of my Baptism has been simply and solely anticipatory of my re-birth into the world to come. I expect to find that what happened then was, not analogous to, but on another plane of life identical with that regeneration of which Our Lord spoke to S. Peter in answer to his question, "What then shall we have?" (S. Matt., xix, 28).

"Else what shall they do which are baptised for the dead, if the dead rise not at all," (I. Cor., xv, 29). About the meaning of these words of S. Paul there has been much difference of opinion. With such difference we are not concerned here and readers can find out all about it, admirably set down in Canon Evans' note on the passage in the Speaker's Commentary. Personally I have no doubt that, from the Greek Fathers Chrysostom, Theodoret, Theophylact, and others to Canon Evans himself, those interpreters have been right who regard it as an elliptical sentence in which the words "for the dead" really mean "with an interest in the resurrection of the dead, with an eye to their resurrection." Baptism itself means nothing unless it means a regeneration anticipatory of our re-birth into the world to come. If there is no resurrection then there is no final re-birth; if there is no final re-birth, then the preliminary one of Baptism has no meaning. This is S. Paul's argument in a nutshell.

The only terms in which I find it possible to conceive my own passing from this world to the next is in the terms of a birth. "If there is a natural body, there is also a spiritual body." My natural body I inherited. It is an admirable but very limiting instrument. It is getting old and wearing out. With it as my instrument I ought to have been making, I hope I have been making, my spiritual body. I shall not be surprised if I find that every good Communion that I have made has actually transmuted some of the natural into some of the spiritual. Many will regard this as superstition; but then most of the things that I live by would be regarded by some folk as superstitious; so I shall continue to live by them all the same.

If, however, I am asked what I mean by my spiritual body, my answer must be that I do not conceive it to be a body made of spirit—which, as I have said, probably means nothing—but rather as the living embryo of my body that is to be in any world to come. Here I inherited my natural body and a great bundle of wonderful faculties; there I expect to be able to make for myself my own instrument for my own self-expression, perhaps not immediately, but progressively after my last and true re-birth.

I shall not be surprised if for a while I live in a dream-world of my own, probably not realising that I have died, to wake up presently—as I woke up some sixty years ago—among friends. I expect to find myself quite definitely somewhere, and somewhere in the same great Universe, in one small corner of which all my experiences have hitherto lain. I expect to find myself *myself*, in spite of having a new instrument or body and in spite of beginning to function in a completely new world. My personal identity will be preserved through this entire change of environment because (and only because) my most proximate environment of all—my own body—will be my very own. I shall make it or grow it for myself out of what I carry over. Herein lies the essential truth of the resurrection of the body. On it depends the conserving of personal identity. If I was suddenly given a brand new body in a totally unfamiliar world, I might be a very interesting person to myself and others, but I should be no longer I.

If in this world I reached the point in my evolution at which I could pass on by transfiguration, then I expect that there would be the same unbroken continuity between my this world's instrument of expression and my next world's instrument of expression, as there seems to have been between Our Lord's pre and post resurrection bodies. He was normal and I am still abnormal. His Body disappeared from the tomb and mine will not. He deliberately underwent the experience of death; I cannot avoid it. Hence I need to be born again into the next world as He did not. He was at once here or there at will.

On either side of the picture of the Resurrection on a window in our cloister at Chester the artist has painted two butterflies. It is a happy touch. The transformation of the chrysalis into the butterfly has always seemed to men a sort of natural analogy of the resurrection. I think I should call it an identity on another plane, especially with our modern knowledge as to the actual process of the transformation. I believe that I am right in saying that most of a chrysalis consists of material out of which a tiny sort of central nervous ganglion actually constructs or somehow directs the construction of the butterfly or other insect. If this is so, it illustrates exactly what I conceive we carry on with us at death, a spiritual body, corresponding to the nervous centre of the chrysalis, together with something—perhaps best thought of as potential energy of character—out of which we shall ourselves begin to construct an instrument wherewith to function in the manifold spaciousness of the world to come. As I have said, I expect to wake up among friends who will help and take care of me during the infant days of my eternal life as they did when I was born here according to the flesh and re-born, after the Spirit, on the great day of my own baptism. I hope another day myself to welcome and take care of others when they come along.

III.

When during our long approach to this thinking about the life of the world to come we considered some of biology's findings as to life in this present world, certain features stood out. From its start and throughout the whole process and progress of life some output of energy, in response to some sort of appetency, has been requisite. More and more freedom has been won by increase of faculty and increasing individuality has always meant a multiplication of relationships. I see no reason to suppose that these outstanding features of life disappear on the higher plane which opens out for us after our re-birth into the world to come.

(1) Life will still mean for us an output of energy. It may be that hereafter we shall find ourselves possessed of unlimited stores of energy—something like radium on our material plane—but I doubt it. I think it much more likely that we shall still have to assimilate energy in some way. Here of course the vegetable world stores it up for us and we take it in the shape of food. Whether hereafter we continue to assimilate energy by process of eating and drinking, I do not propose to speculate, but I expect to find that in some way we are able to absorb and utilise energy still and if there is something in the world to come corresponding to the familiar meals of earth, the world to come will not be the less rich and delightful in consequence. It may be that we too easily allow ourselves to interpret figuratively—"But I say unto you that I will not drink henceforth of this fruit of the vine, until that day when I drink it new with you in my Father's kingdom." (S. Matt., xxvi., 29).

(2) In this world our faculties are truly wonderful; but they are few and limited and our physical bodies confine us to a small corner of the Universe. After our re-birth we begin, I expect, to be cosmic persons, set the amazingly interesting task of winning the freedom of the Universe itself by unlimited increase of faculty. I see no reason to suppose that faculty can be made hereafter otherwise than it is made here, that is by the exercise of energy which we have made our own; only hereafter there will be no hampering sickness or still more hampering sin. It should be an altogether delightful going on and on with more and more wonder and worship.

I do not expect to find myself in what I might call a thin sort of world. All of beauty and truth and goodness that has been able to be expressed in our physical world is surely going to be conserved. It is to greater and not to less glories of the Universe to which we shall be admitted, if we attain that world at all. When preachers suggest that the one thing we ought to want is to have done with symbols and shows in order that we may revel in a sort of spiritual intellectualism, I always begin to think about something else. I do not look forward to a thin world at all, but to a very thick one, in which I shall be able to sense, throughout their total scales, vibrations of air and electricity and ether, and to function at will, it may be, on other great worlds, which are not really, I imagine, merely put up in the sky to amuse us through our telescopes. I see no reason to suppose that this winning of the freedom of the Universe by increase of faculty will not take time, or, perhaps it is better to say, make time. Change makes time and without time there can be neither growth or development in any world anywhere. I expect that there will be any amount of time and that we shall count it differently from the sometimes hurried and sometimes tedious measures of earth. At any rate my Expecto looks into a world of inexhaustible interest and unlimited ability.

(3) In this world, if we have achieved any survival value, we have begun to be individuated by multiplying our relationships—we have begun to love the brother whom we have seen. Evolution chose for her driving force in this direction the love of husband and wife with the gift of children. I expect to find all its results conserved, and to find that the sort of love that has been my most precious possession in my own home is the sort of love which, with all its joys and none of its sorrows, widens out its embrace to include, not one small circle, but the whole great family of the eternal Father. For this to be possible, we shall have to become much larger persons than we know ourselves to be on earth. Here the wider our affections, the thinner they are apt to become.

I expect also that our powers of communicating with each other in the world to come will be infinitely extended; but I do not expect to find myself in a sort of ocean of amiably fluidic and interpenetrating thought. I take it that the whole meaning of the whole great process of organic evolution is the making of individual persons in order that individual persons may be re-born into the world to come. A general and universal interpenetration of thought would seem to me to be the destruction of individual personality and likely to be both uninteresting and inconvenient. But I do expect to find quite unlimited facilities for intercourse between individual persons and mutual delight in such intercourse. In all directions we shall, I imagine, need each other's help, and the delight of giving and receiving will be the same. At any rate, I say again, my Expecto looks into a world of wonderful love and happiness.

IV.

I expect to find that I carry on with me very much which is incompatible with life and love in the world to come and that it will have to be destroyed. I do not hope to escape altogether from that in the Universe which is figured by eternal fire. But I think that it will be a fire of purification and not of endless and futile penalty. "They that have done evil will go into everlasting fire;" but unless, when their ungodliness is taken away there is nothing left, something purified and very precious will come out again. By what methods our selfishness, pettinesses, jealousies, our sloths and indifference will be disciplined out of us I cannot foresee at all; but it does seem to me clear that all that a soul or self carries on with it, which is incongruous with the large and sweet and progressive life of the world to come, must be eliminated and I expect that the process of elimination is a painful one. In not a few cases the total self may cease to be.

I expect to find that it is either undesirable or that it is extraordinarily difficult, if not impossible, at the present stage of things, to communicate with the conscious minds of those who are still in the flesh; but I expect to have some consciousness of their thoughts as far as their thoughts are directed towards me. But I do not expect to be able to read their thoughts unless they are directed towards me. Birth into a new world may render me more telepathic but it cannot make me omniscient. If, of their charity, they pray for me, I expect that I shall be aware of it and also aware of its helpfulness. I expect to find that, during my own earth life, I was being greatly helped by the prayers of those who before me reached the other side and that many good things, which seemed to reach me from the depths of my sub-conscious, originated from friends who loved me here and love still. I am afraid that I shall find many who were hurt and disappointed by the ease and rapidity with which I forgot them and I hope that I may find ways to make amends. I expect to find that one of the delights of the life of the world to come will be the possibility of helping with the making of their selves those who have been left behind, by energies of thought and prayer. I see no reason to expect that I shall be aware of their circumstances and experiences; but I do expect that, as far as I am aware, many things, that would have distressed me much on earth will look quite all right from the other side.

In an earlier chapter of this book the view has been expressed that our physical brain is the instrument which obliges us to concentrate our attention on one particular earth life; that it is the instrument which compels us to forget rather than the instrument which enables us to remember. When hereafter I am able to function without a physical brain, I expect to find that the experiences which have led to my being what I am are vastly greater than I had supposed. I hope, indeed, to find that I shall be able to recall and to retain in memory the whole of those age-long experiences, which were condensed into the faculties I inherited at my birth on earth and to know the whole of my history, not scientifically from the outside, but from the inside as stages through which I have passed in the making of the being which I find myself to be, with a future, compared with which the vastness of my past is inconsiderable. Already I know that I have cost the travail of a world and of its Author to the uttermost, and my Expecto would be unworthy were it not hopefully immense.

"That God may be all in all"—the most comprehensive statement of the whole purpose comes to us from S. Paul. How he began to think it out or whether he began to think it out at all, I do not know. But it seems to me that if what I seem to see in front turns out to be true, then S. Paul's forecast of the great purpose will be indeed fulfilled. When all those who have taken up their "right to become children of God" see themselves from start to finish as He sees them; when, as the outcome, they restore to Him His freedom laid aside by Him for a season that they might win the liberty of the glory of the children of God; when the knowledge of all is the knowledge of God and when their wills are His will; then literally and fully God will be all in all for ever and ever.

V.

The travail of a world—a living world, personal from end to end; its every law an act of will, its every aspect the aspect of a Person. "The physicist looks at the data and says, 'It is all law,' the philosopher ponders them and concludes, 'It is all mind': but the greatest induction is that of the man who has lived through it all, noting the resultant of the various sequences in the case of his own experience, and who can truthfully say at the end, 'It is all love'." So writes Professor Simpson and it could not be better put. Religion is the synthesis of all three—law, mind, love, personally experienced and progressively apprehended. To present it as such has been the purpose of this book. But I expect that in the world to come the personal aspect will fill the view and that

I shall find that I have thought most truly of this present world when it has been to me the Self-expression of One of Whom I think least inadequately when I worship Him as Three Persons in One God.

"In the beginning was the Word, and the Word was with God, and the Word was God . . . . He was in the world, and the world was made by him and the world knew him not . . . . And the Word became flesh and dwelt among us (and we beheld his glory, glory as of the only begotten of the Father) full of grace and truth." (S. John I., 1, 10, 14). It is in the world of which He is the Conscious Energy, in ourselves and in our neighbours of whom He is the best Self, that we must recognise Him if we are to find Him at all, and He is not far to seek.

"I see His Blood upon the rose,
And in the stars the glory of His eyes:
His body gleams amid eternal snows,
His tears fall from the skies.

I see His Face in every flower;
The thunder and the singing of the birds
Are but His voice—and carven by His power
Rocks are His written words.

All pathways by His Feet are worn,
His strong Heart stirs the ever-beating sea,
His Crown of thorns is twined with every thorn,
His Cross is every tree."*

---

* By kind permission of the widow of the author, Joseph Mary Plunkett.

For most of us in this present world such lines—the beauty and strength of which we can hardly help feeling—are an exaggeration. Only sometimes do we see these things, when we are at our occasional very best. I expect that in the world to come we shall find that they are more than literally true of all the time. "We shall see Him as He is." This is part of my Expecto; but when or where or how I do not know and will not try to guess.

VI.

No one can even begin to read the great book of Evolution and miss the outstanding lesson that for any sort of progress, for any getting forward, there must be on the part of organism or person some output of energy, motived by some sort of appetency, with something like faith and some kind of self committal.

It seems at least unlikely that anyone will survive into any world to come who does not want to. Many things combine in many cases to make men only too willing to seek equilibrium here and to live their whole lives with no thought of any beyond, let alone any desire for one. Faith is the highest activity of life and sometimes we have not life enough in us to exercise it. Few of us escape altogether from times when we simply don't care. Not seldom serious illness brings such a time; all our energy is gone. And, if we are quite contented with this world and want no other, need we blame ourselves? If we prefer to be failures, what does it matter? If we wish for no further life, why should we not have our wish?

If we were living in an impersonal Universe there would, I think, be no answer—no reason why a man should strive if effort was not to his liking. Effort is not to the liking of a great many of us and many grow tired as years advance.

In some cases, no doubt, the wish to survive is a strong motive; in many it is not; in none is it, I think, the true and right one. The true and right motive is lest we fail in our response to a great appeal. We have cost so much, not figuratively, but really. We cannot for shame be failures and disappoint. We have cost the travail of a world; we have cost the self-sacrifice to the uttermost of Him Who made it and us—we know that it is our worse self that flags and hesitates and not our best, and sometimes, at any rate, we are at our best.

In a little Somerset Churchyard lies the body of a great Dean of S. Paul's, of half a century ago, beneath a very modest stone. Round it and by his wish are carved the Latin words of a great old hymn:

Quaerens me, sedisti lassus:
Redemisti, crucem passus:
Tantus labor non sit cassus.

So great labour let it not be in vain—surely this is the prayer for us all when we know that we are down upon our lees, when equilibrium tempts us to abandon effort, when we are in danger of the only possible failure in the Christian life—the failure of ceasing to try. Then "Let it not be in vain that Thou hast died."

* * * *

More than once as I have been writing this adventurous book, the old saying about fools rushing in where angels fear to tread has suggested itself. I have not, however, rushed. I have put down the very deliberate thinkings of a lifetime on many problems about which I am still, I hope, being renewed day by day in the spirit of my mind. It may be that discussion arising out of this book will make some things clearer to me than they have yet become. About these things I am sure that we all do well to think. I have written rather to provoke thought and, if it may be, to arouse appetency, than to secure agreement with my speculations. It is far better to risk making mistakes than never to think beyond the grave at all. Never to think beyond the grave may make the grave the end. What I have written should disturb no one's faith and ought to diminish no one's hopes, and so I will dare to add

Benedictus benedicat
Per Jesum Christum Dominum nostrum.

INDEX.

Absolution, 108 (note).
Antiquity of Man, 76.
Appetency, 48, 159, 101.
Armagh, Archbishop of, 5.
Arnold, Sir Edwin, 141.
Ascension, The, 109.
Avebury, Lord, 67.

Baptism, 143, 154.
Bergson, M., 1, 20, 24, 27, 37, 75.
Biology, 43.
Blewett, Professor, 59.
Body, The Resurrection of the, 40, 157.
Brain, The, 75, 164.
Brewster, Mr. E. T., 14.

Catholic, 39, 137.
Christianity, 137, 143.
Church and Evolution, The, 130.
Communion of Saints, The, 149.
Comte, Auguste, 27.
Continuity, 59.
Coué, Monsieur, 144.
Cross, The, 85, 87, 88, 104, 136–138, 140.

D'Arcy, Archbishop, 41.
Darwin, 41, 69.
Destruction, 121.
Divorce, 133.
Drummond, Professor Henry, 5, 56.
Du Bose, Dr., 100.

Eternal Punishment, 123–125, 162.
Ether, The, 71.
Eucharist, The, 142.
Evolution, 42.

Faculty, 66, 68.
Faith, 148.
Fall, The, 86.
Fast before Communion, The, 138.
Fosdick, Dr., 8.
Freedom, Development of, 51, 102, 108.
Freewill, 18.

Gore, Bishop, 94, 137.

Hadfield, Dr., 18.
Herman, Mrs. E., 137, 140.
Hymns, 50.

Incarnation, The, 127, 136, 151.
Incense, 139.
Individuality, Growth of, 55.
Infant Baptism, 145.
Instinct, 66–68.
Isaiah, 29.

James, Professor William, 12.

Karma, 90, 91.

Lodge, Sir Oliver, 7, 32, 70.
Lubbock, Sir John, 67.

Magic, 146.
Marriage, 131, 133, 134.
Material World, Object of, 36, 37.

McDowall, Mr., 36, 72, 129.
McNeile, Dr. A. H., 38, 81, 123, 125.
Mediæval Outlook, 11.
Mystery, A., 135.
Mystery Religions, 137.

Nature, A law of, 14, 85.

Otto, Rudolph, 88.

S. Paul, 44, 87, 90, 111, 112, 115, 125, 126, 130, 131, 164.
Personal Identity, 153.
Plunkett, Joseph Mary, 166.
Prayer, 22–26.

Regeneration, 154.
Re-incarnation, 68, 70, 71, 80, 89, 90.
Religion, Difficulty of, 49.
Resurrection, The, 107, 108, 113, 136.
Re-union, 149.

Sacraments, 141, 144, 146, 147.
Salvation, 90.
Self, 79, 80, 122, 128.
Simpson, Professor J. Y., 2, 3, 14, 20, 23, 30, 41, 42, 44 51, 53, 55, 61, 72, 76, 77, 85, 91, 101, 121, 129, 141 152, 165.
Speaker's Commentary, 155.
Spirit, The Holy, 93, 94–96.
Spiritual Body, 116, 156.
Spiritualism, 81–83.
Studdert-Kennedy, Rev. G. A., 143.
Sub-conscious, The, 81.
Swete, Dr., 95.
Symbols, 148.

Theology, 44, 59.
Thomson, Professor J. Arthur, 2, 29, 57, 59, 63, 64, 72.
Transfiguration, The, 33, 104–106, 152.

Universalism, 91, 92.

Virgin Birth, The, 96–100.

Westcott, Bishop, 7, 15, 35, 95, 151.
Weymouth, Dr., 93, 111, 112, 115.